29 95

D0939387

Target Editing

I dedicate this book to my son, Craig--
May our family's table talk about writing
make you a successful editor.

Target Editing

Quick VanWrite Revisions
Energize Business Writing

by

Linda Vanderwold

VanWrite Publishers
Davis, California

Target Editing! Copyright © 1995 by Linda Vanderwold. Printed and bound in the United States of America. All rights reserved. No part of this book may be reproduced in any form or by any electronic or mechanical means including information storage and retrieval systems without permission in writing from the publisher, except by a reviewer, who may quote brief passages in a review to be printed in a magazine or newspaper.

Published by
VanWrite Publishers
PO Box 4414
Davis, California 95617-4414

1-800-800-0898
VanWrite@aol.com

Corporate America is increasingly aware of the expense associated with poor writing. The author and publisher merely suggest a workable method to achieve clear writing. In no way are these suggestions mandatory or exhaustive. Prudent writers will incorporate these suggestions in a manner compatible with their corporate culture.

Library of Congress Cataloging-in-Publication Data

Vanderwold, Linda B.

   Target Editing quick VanWrite revisions energize business writing   Includes index.
   1. English language--Composition and exercises 2. English language--Business English.   I. Title

PE1483.V15   808.06665

Library of Congress Catalog Card Number: 94-90019

ISBN 0-9639282-0-1

10 9 8 7 6 5 4 3 2 1

Acknowledgments

Target Editing grew out of repeated requests from my seminar participants that I write a book to capture the gems of our seminars. My audience/students include executives and middle management career professionals in both the public and private sectors.

I want to thank all those seminar participants for their interest in and application of the VanWrite method. Also, I thank all the professional business people who brought their work writing to our seminars and offered it as fair game in our discussions about weak and strong writing. We all benefitted from the synergy! In addition, I thank:

Benjamin F. Dover, an entrepreneur, popular talkradio host, a successful writer, and my mentor;

Jim Donovan, my editor; his edits furthered the book's clarity and standardized its presentation;

Denise Arend, a good friend I met at a VanWrite seminar; she owns a very successful consulting firm. Denise studied the first draft and provided many valuable tips;

Alan Criswell, a fine thinker at the Office of the State Controller, State of California; during a VanWrite seminar, Alan contributed many fine ideas when I mentioned I was open to suggestions for a title that conveyed what I taught;

Kevin Bacon, a Principal at Price Waterhouse LLP, who advanced the growth of VanWrite;

Kim Bacon, who encouraged me to blaze a new career path in the late 1980s;

Karin and Leonard Berglund, my parents, and JoAnn and Paul Berglund, aunt and uncle, who cheered and supported me in many ways;

My husband Fred, who lovingly assumed the major parenting role of our son Craig while I gave birth to **Target Editing**

Most of all, I want to thank my "breathing coaches" throughout this labor, my best buddies SW and DL.

What people say about VanWrite:

"Linda delivers an excellent program. I saw immediate improvement in my writing skills and in my comfort with writing. Linda's examples are from the "real world," and her presentation is powerful yet refreshingly simple. Her professionalism and enthusiastic personality make learning the VanWrite Method fun."

> *Margaret O'Sullivan*
> *Senior Account Representative,*
> *HealthCare COMPARE*

"VanWrite is the best writing seminar I ever took! It's exciting because I applied the method immediately and saw great results."

> *Bev Sherman*
> *Staff System Analyst*
> *Teale Data Center*

"Using VanWrite, I finally learned HOW to make writing better. Linda explains each idea clearly, and then demonstrates how to use it in your daily writing tasks. I cannot say enough about the value of this method for anybody who writes."

> *Alice Jones*
> *Manager*
> *Department of General Services*
> *State of California*

"*Target Editing* sets a new standard for books about writing. This useful book is for working people who frequently write on their jobs."

> *Benjamin Dover*
> *Talkradio Host, 570 KLIF AM*
> *Dallas, Texas*

"All business writers strive for clear communication; the VanWrite method provides practical, simple, yet powerful guidelines to insure that each staff member produces focused, readable documents."

> *Michael Burke*
> *National Sales and Marketing Director*
> *Superior Farms, Inc.*

"Once VanWrite gets in your head, you never forget it."

> *Elosia Stratton*
> *CEO, Strategic Planning,*
> *Department of General Services*
> *State of California*

"VanWrite is an easy editing method that helps any writer achieve clarity quickly."

> *Rick Pomeroy*
> *Program Supervisor*
> *Secondary Teacher Education*
> *University of California, Davis*

Contents

Introduction:
Who Needs Color?
The VanWrite Method

Does writing cause you stress? Do you ever hate to write? Do you rewrite countless times and still feel dissatisfied? Then this book is for you. **Target Editing** presents the VanWrite Method, a very simple approach to writing that enables you to understand how a sentence communicates, or why it does not, and how to improve it.

The VanWrite Method reviews and pivots on just a few basic grammatical concepts that make your business writing successful. As a business writer, you must be attentive to a few elements of grammar to be in control of your writing. Cooks know the impact of particular spices on the flavor of a dish; similarly, if you pay attention to the placement of subject, verb, and prepositional phrases, you control the flavor of your writing and avoid creating unclear bureaucratic documents. Most importantly, this approach to writing reduces the stress you experience about writing, and gives you control of your sentences so you say what you mean.

Most writers can identify several elements of grammar, but they tend to think of grammar as apart from or unrelated to writing. Anybody who writes needs to be conversant with the basic grammatical elements of a sentence. **Target Editing** presents grammar in living color! This book shows you how to apply grammar to the writing process. We do this through the use of color to highlight the key elements in any sentence. Pink, blue, and green (traditionally the colors for girls, boys, and money) indicate a strong sentence in active voice that tells *who did what:*

On Tuesday, staff raised several issues.

Conversely, a sentence with lots of yellow and orange will be wordy, unclear, and weak:

A number (of issues) were raised by the staff on Tuesday.

In my seminars I always ask business writers what they remember about the grammar instruction they had in school. In response I hear, "I never think about it," or "I always hated grammar," or "I don't worry about it because I know how to write complete sentences."

Teachers spend considerable time discussing grammar, but beyond the complete sentence, somehow students neglect to make the connection between grammar and clear writing. If business writers ignore the basics of grammar, they surrender their control over the sentences they write! This book presents no brand new ideas about grammar; rather, it reviews and refreshes what you were taught years ago. Then the book teaches the VanWrite editing method so you can apply that knowledge to your writing to be successful every time.

Today no business or organization can afford to be misunderstood in writing. Also, no business can afford to have employees spend inordinate amounts of time revising, or worse, rewriting. Finally, the revision process sometimes feels fruitless because the writer tends to focus only on content, with little thought to clarity and presentation.

The VanWrite Method color code functions much like the multiplication tables. We used the tables regularly when we were learning arithmetic, but now we refer to them only subconsciously. Similarly, business writers trained in the VanWrite Method use highlighter pens regularly when they are learning the system to make abstract grammar visually clear. Then, an experienced VanWriter will read a document quickly without highlighting it and say, "I see a lot of yellow and orange here; I don't see any blue or green." These comments refer to the reader's mental picture of the writing's clarity. This occurs because readers visualize color much more easily than they think about grammatical concepts.

Target Editing reviews only those grammatical concepts necessary for clear business writing; then this book teaches you to visualize those elements in color so you edit effectively. For example, the book dis-cusses sentence style, sentence length, and the importance of verb choice for concise business writing. The VanWrite Method enables you to approach writing tasks, as writer or editor, very effectively and objectively. However, this book is **not** about grammar; instead, it is about effective business writing. When you write effectively, you are efficient; similarly, when you employ concrete, objective, consistent edits with your staff, you also save time, money, and emotional energy. People trained in the VanWrite Method report permanent, positive changes in their writing; repeatedly they mention the simplicity of the concept and how easy it is to implement. Some writers seem almost annoyed that no one taught them this approach in school!

In this book, the sample business sentences are authentic; they come from real-life business documents participants brought to VanWrite seminars. After you study this book you will not need to rewrite your work documents from scratch. Instead, you will make targeted revisions using the VanWrite

Method. You will identify and preserve your strong energetic passages. Simultaneously, you will target the weak areas and easily edit to increase your document's clarity and vigor. Once you bring the VanWrite colors to your editing, you will wonder how you functioned in only black and white!

Target Editing

Chapter **1**

Sidebars:

In this sidebar area, periodically I present definitions of terms used in the main text, or occasional editorial comments. This area can also serve as a "wake-up call"--are you with me? I invite you to use this space to jot notes to yourself.

Briefly, *Target Editing*

presents a simple concept-- choose your subject and verb (i.e. actor and action) very carefully! Chapter 2 explains subject and verb in detail. This

The Black and White of Writing
That's the Way It's Always Been

Whenever a *reader* has to reread a sentence to understand the message, the *writer* has failed to communicate effectively. In your hands you hold the simplest method to clarify your business writing style. As soon as you begin studying this easy method you will understand why the following very bureaucratic sentence begs to be ignored in offices across America:

The purpose of this memo is to explain parking.

Chapter 2 discusses the weaknesses in this sentence, and presents a concrete edit: *This memo explains parking.* Then the book teaches you an objective revision approach you can apply universally to all your writing. Once you master the concepts, you will edit with greatly increased confidence and minimal effort.

Many books exist to help the business writer, but most are academic in presentation and go into more grammatical detail than you want. **Target Editing** emphasizes targeted revising rather than wholesale rewriting. By example and demonstration, this approach is not abstract, and it answers our most basic question: *Who did that?*

Juxtapose:

to place side by side

objective concepts

means you utilize these techniques according to specified, regular standards. As the writer or editor, you easily measure the increased clarity each time you revise a sentence using the VanWrite Method.

You need highlighter pens

in the colors suggested by the chapter titles.

editing approach focuses on three simple concepts; in every sentence

juxtapose *Subject and Verb*

to answer *Who Did What*

and to increase *Reader Comfort.*

Our basic editing premise maintains that content is fine, but the presentation will gain strength when you revise according to the VanWrite Method.

Target Editing holds the discussion of grammatical concepts to the bare minimum, presenting only objective concepts that will apply each time you employ them, either as writer or editor. For high visual impact you'll use highlighter pens to identify key elements in a sentence; the colors enable you to recognize easily those elements that reinforce clarity and Reader Comfort, and those elements that do not.

This book assumes you have precious little time for revision. VanWrite's objective editing method allows you to edit your own or another's writing expediently without changing the style or voice. All your edits aim at the three concepts above. You gain *conscious* control over skills you use everyday in your writing tasks; best of all, the concrete, transferable

Has this ever happened to you?

Or, have you ever made an unexplained comment on another's writing? Recall the sinking feeling when you don't like a document but you don't know why.

The writer might even make the document worse!

An office runs most smoothly when all writers subscribe to the VanWrite Method; then all staff can talk to each other objectively about editing.

Reader Comfort

increases comprehension; when a reader feels less threatened, that reader is more open to suggestion.

techniques take the guesswork out of what makes good writing.

Often business writers say they do not understand why their managers suggest many of the edits they do. Many business writers lack a clear set of objective techniques to use in the editing process. Frequently managers tell staff, "Keep working on this; it is not quite what I want." This vague direction only results in vague editing. Yes, the writer will make changes, but with no guarantee that the edits will yield any improvement *because* the writer received no clear directives. The VanWrite Method provides objective and measurable techniques; they are *not* based on individual preference or style. Instead, the suggestions apply to all writing tasks and can be employed by all staff levels.

The VanWrite Method maintains Reader Comfort as the writer's overall goal/concern. The concept sounds rather generous and humanitarian, but in reality it's more self-serving. Frequently writers feel so much pressure to produce that they fail to consider the most important party of all--the poor victim who has to read and then respond to the particular document. Writers feel bogged down with their own worries-- deadlines, boss's happiness, overall work load. Sure, writers attend to the audience/reader regarding the

When a reader feels comfortable, the reader is more likely to be agreeable and willing to consider the writer's point.

reader's knowledge of the topic; however, writers often neglect to monitor their writing in terms of Reader Comfort to insure that the reader follows the prose effortlessly or painlessly.

Too many times writers sabotage their own good ideas by burying them in bureaucratic style and making the reader uncomfortable. Uncomfortable readers choose to ignore the writing that makes them work too hard; that's the letter that goes to the bottom of the pile, or the request that receives an immediate negative response. Even worse, the reader tends to make a judgment about the writer's intellect! As Albert Camus said, "Bad writing has commentators. Good writing has readers." Human nature reacts similarly in all arenas; when we are comfortable, we are more affirmative/positive, but when we are uncomfortable, we respond negatively. If writers pay attention to Reader Comfort, they produce documents that achieve the results they want; comfortable readers tend to connect with, or at least willingly consider, your message.

Readers develop a positive mindset about and a high level of confidence in the writer who communicates well. The best test of easy communication is reading down the page; reading is a downward movement. When the reader needs to read UP the

Ward Cleaver retired!

The old academic protocol maintained that more is better; these are lean years! Today, we write to communicate, not to confuse or confound. Now, less is more!

page--i.e., put a finger on the period and go in search of the beginning--the writer has failed to communicate. In the business world, readers subconsciously base many decisions on their emotional reaction to the writer's style; clear writing reflects clear thinking, while unclear writing suggests that the writer is uneasy with the topic. Without even realizing it, readers make these decisions based on their comfort level.

The VanWrite Method emphasizes techniques that reinforce the Reader Comfort concept. This book explains how sentence style relates to message. ***Target Editing*** demonstrates how sentence length affects Reader Comfort and how writers mistakenly *add* words to already confusing sentences in a vain attempt to clarify their message. In addition, an important VanWrite element focuses on how verb choice enlivens or deadens a sentence. Then, paragraph unity and coherence demonstrate the importance of fulfilling the mental expectations (verbal contract) the writer gave the reader in the topic sentence.

I have presented this method in seminars to hundreds of business people; 98% marvel at how much easier writing and editing became once they utilized the VanWrite Method. Simultaneously, these people

Enjoy your book!

Believe it or not, you will find this quite painless, even fun!

Prose:

Everyday writing, opposed to verse or rhyme. (It has nothing to do with sports.)

Write on!

Soon you will uncap your pens and paint your way to clear business writing.

became critical of writing that failed to measure up to their new standards for clarity. I kept this colorful book brief because the Method is very simple. Also, I kept this book brief because clear, concise writing is brief.

If it's been forever since you consciously juggled grammar, blaze through Chapters 2, 3, and 4 to re-familiarize yourself with the concepts. After you do the initial read-through, go back to ponder the prose and to study the examples. Chapters 5, 6, and 7 introduce no new material; instead, they illustrate the colors of clarity with detailed, friendly discussions of specific edits. After you internalize the concepts in Chapters 2, 3, and 4, and study the examples in Chapters 5, 6, and 7, you will delight in your new writing confidence!

2

Chapter

State of Being:

A verb that conveys no action, for example: *is, am, are, was, were, be, being, been.* These verbs refer to existence or state of being only. "I *am* short." "He *is* sick." Don't panic... Chapter 3 discusses verbs in depth.

Actor/Subject:

In this book we use actor and subject interchangeably to identify the person or thing that acts/performs the action.

The **Pink** and Yellow of Writing
Who Did What?

In this chapter we examine the power that writers have when they select their subject(s) and verb(s) carefully. Subject and verb selection addresses both word choice **and** word placement within each sentence. In any editing endeavor, you must focus on one sentence at a time. Here we go with our brief review of necessary grammar! Within an individual sentence, *subject and verb* form the key elements. How do you find them in a sentence? EASY! Start with the verb; ask yourself, *"What is the action or state of being in this sentence?"* This question yields the verb. Then ask yourself, *"Who or what did/does it?"* This question identifies the subject or actor. When you analyze a sentence, always underline <u>subject</u> once and <u>verb</u> twice to reference these important elements.

Study these examples:

I went to the store. What's the action here? **went.** Who/What went? **I.** <u>I</u> <u>went</u> to the store.

Their company hosts many off-site meetings.
Action? **hosts**; who hosts? **company** hosts. Their company <u>hosts</u> many off-site meetings.

Pink: *Very Desirable*

To write a clear sentence, always choose the word in subject position very carefully. In a good sentence the grammatical subject presents the topic of the sentence. In addition, the subject and the verb lend more wallop in a sentence when they are **juxtaposed**, i.e., they are positioned side by side to answer *who did what* quickly. We use the pink marker to highlight juxtaposed subject/verb. Look at the difference between these two (very elementary) sentences included in a press release:

The <u>maintenance workers</u> <u>pruned</u> the trees in City Park.

The <u>trees</u> in City Park <u>were pruned</u> by the maintenance workers.

In the first, the actors performed an action; this is a good sentence in a paragraph on the maintenance workers because it focuses the reader's attention *on*

Subject position:

What the heck is that? Simply, that means the writer should make the *actor* the doer in the sentence; for example, in the following sentence the actor/human is not the grammatical subject:

<u>Barking</u> <u>was heard</u> by the neighbors.

A better sentence puts the human actor as the grammatical subject:

The <u>neighbors</u> <u>heard</u> barking.

Prepare to see the word **juxtapose** frequently, one of the primary concepts of the VanWrite Method.

Except--

As with any "rule" or practice in English, an exception pops up immediately! Regarding subject-verb juxtapositioning, the exception includes words (adverbs) that tell time, such as *always, never,* or *rarely.* These words work best between subject and verb, as illustrated below:

I always take my lunch to work.

If you move *always* around in the sentence, the construction sounds strained.

The maintenance workers never pruned the trees.

Again, the sentence would be awkward if we put *never* at the end in an effort to juxtapose subject and verb.

Solution--

So what do we do about this? We bend the rule! Include *always* and *never* in your blaze of **pink.** Generally (!) speaking, the rule bends no further than this.

the topic, maintenance workers. Readers subconsciously expect the word in subject position to be the focus of the sentence. This sentence answers the question *Who did what?* Moreover, business readers read only for information--they want to know *who did what.* In the first sentence we highlight the subject and verb in **pink** because they are juxtaposed, a strong quality.

The **maintenance workers pruned** the trees in City Park.

What makes a good actor/subject? Whenever possible, use a person or a concrete noun. Choose an actor capable of action. Ideally, choose an actor (a *who*) with a heartbeat. In the first sentence **maintenance workers** are capable of many actions. In the second sentence **trees** do nothing alone; they only exist. The actors are hidden in the prepositional phrase (defined in a moment) and the writer asks the reader to focus on the concept of trees.

Furthermore, in concert with the Total Quality Management (TQM) wave sweeping across government and private industry, organizations now see the value in naming/identifying the actor; people are interested in other people. We want credit when we deserve it, and we like to feel that others take responsibility when necessary. Classic bureaucratic writing is falling out of favor at last! Readers want specific information, and they want it communicated clearly.

The second sentence is a good sentence in a paragraph on the **trees** in City Park:

The <u>trees</u> in City Park <u>were pruned</u> by the maintenance workers.

The pruning was done by the maintenance workers, and the planting was done by the Friends of the Arboretum, etc. However, the second sentence is a lousy sentence in a paragraph on the maintenance workers because I put the focus on the trees; unwittingly, I confused my reader by sloppy word choice in subject position. To answer *Who did what?* my reader has to go through mental gymnastics, not fair of me to require! In short, Reader Comfort is low.

A sentence contains subject and verb, and expresses a complete thought; most sentences include phrases, all include independent clauses, and many include dependent clauses. Before you protest that this is getting too technical, consider this: research tells us speed readers skip or at best scan prepositional phrases and dependent clauses; therefore, in the business setting no writer wants to position the

Phrase:

A group of words that does not contain both subject and verb. The VanWrite Method focuses on the prepositional phrase because many writers use it carelessly. *Target Editing* uses the shorter term "prep phrase" to refer to prepositional phrases.

Clause:

A group of words that contains both subject and verb. You're right; this sounds like the definition of a sentence. Later in this chapter we will discuss the clause in more detail.

Noun and Pronoun:

No matter how technically advanced we become, some things never change. Recall your elementary teachers' definitions of noun and pronoun. **Noun** is a person, place, thing, quality, or concept. **Pronoun** substitutes for a noun (no, it's not a noun that has gone professional). Appendix A provides a simple pronoun chart, and reviews how to use pronouns correctly.

topic or main actor/agent in a construction (such as prep phrase or dependent clause) many readers skip!

Yellow: Caution

Let's resume the discussion of phrase and clause, prepositional phrase first. Phrases exist for every part of speech (e.g., noun phrases, adjective phrases), and grammarians discuss such phenomena at parties; we won't! A phrase is a group of words that does not contain both subject and verb. In this book we limit our discussion to the prepositional phrase because it is the phrase out of control in business writing; interestingly, we cannot live without prep phrases because they express relationships, one of the concepts most dear to humans.

Prepositions describe—

> time: *after, before, in*
>
> location: *behind, on, in, beside*
>
> association: *of, with, for, about*
>
> direction: *from, to, between*

A preposition connects a noun or pronoun with some other word in the sentence. This connection/preposition is usually the first word of a short phrase that somehow modifies another idea in the sentence. When we edit we place parentheses around the entire prep phrase to identify it quickly. The subject and verb never appear in the prep phrase. Note the role of the prepositional phrases in the following sentences:

> **The executive staff returned (after the meeting).** (tells when)

> **Managers told staff (about the new policies).** (tells what)

> **I ran (from the car) (to the office).** (two phrases describing association and location)

The English language features about 75 common prepositions, and probably we will not discover any new ones in the late 20th or early 21st centuries. To determine if a word is a prep, use the word in front of the "___ the door": *above, across, along, among, around, before, behind, below, beneath, down, for, from, in, into, inside, over, through, to, toward, under, until, apart from, because of, on account of*—the list goes on.

In the examples above, the prep phrases do not interfere with the subject-verb juxtaposition.

All three sentences tell *who did what* clearly because each juxtaposes Subject and Verb.

S/V splits are one of life's many ironies; in an effort to be more clear, writers actually confuse their readers with too many words.

In these three examples of S/V (subject/verb) split, the word in subject position is weak and has to be qualified, defined, or limited before the writer continues with the verb.

Unfortunately, in business writing prep phrases frequently separate or split subject and verb, greatly reducing Reader Comfort. Most often these subject-verb splits occur because the writer chose a weak actor/subject that needs to be explained or defined before the writer can go ahead with the verb and the rest of the sentence. Note the following examples:

> **The <u>purpose</u> (of this meeting) <u>is</u> . . .**
> **The <u>dimensions</u> (of my office) <u>are</u> . . .**
> **The <u>car</u> (in the parking lot) <u>rolled</u>.**

When this occurs, the writer needs to edit the prep phrase for clarity and Reader Comfort; the writer can choose to relocate the prep phrase, or collapse it and use the information it provides somewhere else in the sentence. This flexibility is illustrated below.

When the prepositional phrase *comes between* subject and verb, we highlight the prep phrase in **yellow.** To monitor Reader Comfort, identify **all** prep phrases by putting parentheses around the phrase(s); then, if a prep phrase interrupts S/V, determine how to move, collapse, or eliminate the phrase in question.

In addition to Reader Comfort, writers need to be attentive to subject/verb placement to avoid grammatical errors. Look at this sentence:

The group (of employees) have no complaints.

What is the action here? **have**. Who or what have no complaints? The **group have**. Oops—*group* is a singular noun requiring a singular verb. The *group* **has** is correct. Because the prep phrase interrupted or separated the subject and verb, the writer made the verb agree with **employees**, the noun in the prep phrase (the object of the prep) and nearest the verb. This common error goes out of every office in America daily when writers do not keep the subject-verb **juxtaposed—side by side.**

What do we do about this common mistake? Reader Comfort increases if you reduce the prep phrase to an adjective and/or move it to the left of the subject whenever possible; thus our example with the blaze of yellow and a grammatical error

The group (of employees) have no complaints.

becomes pink and correct!

The employee group has no complaints. or
The group has no complaints. or
The employees have no complaints.

Object of the prep!?

Relaaax! I offer this academic term for those with strong memories of classroom grammar. "Normal" business writers do not need a working familiarity with the concept.

This edit changes *staff* from a noun in a prep phrase to a single word adjective that modifies the subject. *Members* is a vague subject, evidenced by the fact that it requires a prep phrase of definition before the writer continues with the thought. If we reduce the phrase to an adjective that qualifies *members* initially, we juxtapose the subject & verb. Remember *adjectives*? **Adjectives** describe, limit, or qualify nouns or pronouns: *pretty* eyes, *oak* desk, *beige* carpet. **Adverbs** "advertise" (modify) verbs (<u>ran</u> *quickly*) , adjectives (*extremely* low water level), or other adverbs (ran *very* quickly).

The grammatical subject of a sentence **never** appears in the prep phrase. This is why it is so important to identify the prep phrase(s).

Here is another example of prep phrase editing:

> **All <u>members</u> (of the staff) <u>should read</u> this memo.**

becomes

> **All staff <u>members</u> <u>should read</u> this memo.**

These edits make it easier for the reader to grasp what the writer intends because the writer juxtaposed the subject and verb (arranged them side by side), thereby quickly revealing *who does what*. Reducing prep phrases reduces unnecessary tension in writing; thus, Reader Comfort increases instantly!

Look again at the bureaucratic sentence in Chapter 1:

> **The <u>purpose</u> (of this memo) <u>is</u> to explain parking.**

What is the action or state of being here? **is**; *Who or what **is**?* The **purpose!** So the subject/verb is **purpose is**, but the item the reader has in hand is the memo that explains parking! This discrepancy creates subtle tension in the readers' minds as they try to focus—what is the real issue here, the grammatical subject (the *purpose)* or another topic (*memo*)?

Infinitive?

An infinitive is a verb form not assigned to any actor, preceded by *to—to run, to talk, to drive.* You can distinguish an infinitive from a prep phrase because an infinitive ends with an action word whereas a prep phrase ends with a noun. (Remember being told not to split your infinitives? That meant you should not say *to quickly run;* instead, you would say *to run quickly* because *to run* is the infinitive.)

Is it necessary to tell a reader that a memo has a purpose? Bureaucratic or no, we hope not! Revised to juxtapose subject and verb, to eliminate the prep phrase, *and* to increase Reader Comfort, the sentence reads:

This memo explains parking.

Now this sentence reveals *who did what.* The new concrete grammatical subject came from the prep phrase, and the subject and the topic are now the same word. Wonderful! The strong verb came from the infinitive. We did not rewrite this sentence in the sense that we started over; instead, we revised using the resources already given. The reader will remember this sentence far longer than the original wordier one. Successful business writing requires this level of clarity.

Note this important clue: Anytime the grammatical subject needs to be qualified or defined or explained before the writer continues with the verb, the subject word is too weak. In our example sentence, **purpose** is a weak subject; because the reader immediately asks *purpose of what?*, the writer qualifies the subject with a prep phrase. What is this sentence about? **Memo**, a concrete noun. Again, whenever the grammatical subject and the topic are the same word, the writer utilized a very important concept of clear writing.

The revision

This <mark>memo</mark> <u>explains</u> parking.

reduces word count by 55%, from 9 words to 4!

To reinforce these ideas, in the following sentences examine the underlining and color schemes as they indicate S/V and prep phrase placement. The goal is lots of **pink** and no **yellow.**

Prep phrases that aren't yellow:

We highlight in yellow only those prep phrases that separate the subject and verb. All other prep phrases receive only parentheses to identify them. We want to identify them so we can monitor their use (and avoid overuse).

When other verbiage (garbage?) interrupts subject-verb juxtaposing, underline the interrupter in yellow. See page 31 for an example. In this book yellow is **not** a pretty color; yellow invites confusion because the writer separated the *who* from the *did*. The separation decreases Reader Comfort.

1. <u>We leased</u> a car (with a cellular phone).

This is a good sentence because the S/V are juxtaposed and both are strong. In addition, the sentence answers *who did what.* The prep phrase does not distract the reader; instead, it provides added information. If a speed reader wants to skim the prep phrase, fine--it does not bury an important detail. Remember, you do not want to eliminate prep phrases from your writing because they express relationships; instead, never place the prep phrase(s) between S/V. (Again, you only paint prep phrases **yellow** when they appear between S/V.)

The prep phrase **for a new show** defines the idea.

The prep phrase **in the afternoon** establishes time.

2. **An <u>idea</u> (for a new show) <u>was presented</u> by Tom).**

Although grammatically correct, this sentence lacks Reader Comfort since *who did what* remains unclear until the end. **Idea** is not a good grammatical subject/actor because it requires qualification before the writer proceeds with the verb. This sentence hides the best actor (Tom) in the last prep phrase; draft him to subject position! Revised, the sentence exchanges **yellow** (weak) for **pink** (strong) and answers *who did what:*

> **<u>Tom presented</u> an idea (for a new show).**

3. **The <u>software was installed</u> (in the afternoon).**

Who did that, the ghosts or the gremlins? On first blush this sentence looks good; it paints **pink** because the prep phrase telling time appears at the end. However, the writer neglected to identify an actor capable of action; if we substitute an actor with a heartbeat, we explain *who did what* so the reader experiences no uncertainty:

> **The <u>technicians installed</u> the software (in the afternoon).**

How important is it to identify the actor? *Very* important! Reader Comfort depends on this information. When you identify the actor, although it seems obvious to *you*, you spare the reader even a microsecond of doubt; the reader feels fully informed.

Not too long ago a VanWrite seminar participant told our group that she had prepared her company's latest monthly status report using the VanWrite Method. She noted that the new report was shorter in length but she felt confident that she had conveyed all the necessary news. The next day in a large staff meeting, her manager gave her rave reviews; he commended her for including all the "right information" in this report. Ironically, she had simply revised the report to identify the actors responsible for that month's activities.

Identifying the actors does not require naming them individually, although that practice has merit; it only requires identifying the group, thereby removing the ghosts. This practice is win-win-win; the *writer* feels confident, the *reader* feels very comfortable, and the *workers* feel recognized. The following sentence illustrates this again.

The manager's Reader Comfort was very high. Isn't it interesting that he verbalized his comfort level as accuracy in her writing? No doubt about it—comfortable readers place high confidence in the writer.

This is a "drill": do you feel comfortable with *juxtaposed* S/V? It just means that you place the grammatical subject and the verb next to each other.

4. **Various <u>presentations were chosen</u> (for the trade show).**

Yes, the writer composed a complete sentence and even juxtaposed S/V, but who chose the presentations? **<u>Management</u> <u>chose</u> various presentations for the trade show** provides more Reader Comfort because it identifies *who did what.*

5. **<u>Staff rested</u> (in the lounge) (for 15 minutes) (with their feet up).**

This sentence provides Reader Comfort because the writer juxtaposed S/V **(pink)**, and the reader knows *who did what.* However, note the string of prep phrases. Occasionally you need to move a prep phrase to the front of the sentence so the S/V and *who did what* presentation does not become monotonous or repetitious; in these instances the prep phrase serves as an introductory phrase, thereby breaking the lengthy chain of phrases. As a rule, try to avoid stringing more than two prep phrases together; relocate one phrase to change the pace of the sentence. In this example, any of the prep phrases could move to the front of the sentence easily:

Note the various uses of prep phrases—

these sentences model three prep phrases that each emphasize a different focus and relationship:

In the lounge—location

For 15 minutes—time

With their feet up—how

This edit reduced sentence length by 28%, from 11 words to eight.

(In the lounge), **staff rested** (for 15 minutes) (with their feet up).

(For 15 minutes) **staff rested** (in the lounge) (with their feet up).

(With their feet up), **staff rested** (in the lounge) (for 15 minutes).

Notice that you achieve this difference with targeted revising rather than total rewriting.

6. The **man** (in the red car) **was stopped** (by the police).

Answer the *who did what* question and the logical revision appears:

Police stopped the man (in the red car).

This eliminates the **yellow** and clearly identifies the actor.

7. The **boss hid** (in his office) (under his desk).

This sentence paints **pink,** but it includes consecutive phrases. You could move the first prep phrase to the front of the sentence because it establishes the general location; the second phrase tells the *specific* location:

(In his office,) the <u>boss</u> <u>hid</u> (under his desk).

Clause

The seven preceding sentences illustrated the importance of Subject/Verb selection and placement for the clarity and comfort of any sentence. In short, ***everything depends on the Subject and Verb!*** Remember too, you must use prep phrases carefully. Now we will discuss clause, your final concern in sentence construction.

A **clause** is of a group of words that **contains both subject and verb**. Regarding sentence construction, we label clauses either **independent** or **dependent**.

An **independent clause** (or main clause) can stand alone to express a complete thought.

<u>I</u> <u>enjoyed</u> last night's presentation.

A **dependent clause** (or subordinate clause) cannot stand alone, but helps to express a complete thought when it is attached to a main clause. To identify the dependent clause, enclose it in brackets [ ]. All

The subject and verb express *who does what* in every sentence; make sure you have a good **who!**

Remember fragments?

Lots of fragments are dependent clauses; they contain subject and verb, but they do not express a complete thought. They **depend** on the independent clause in the sentence to clarify them: *Because <u>today</u> <u>is</u> Monday... When <u>I</u> <u>go</u> home... While <u>I</u> <u>finish</u> this letter...*

Subordinating Conjunction:

A word used to begin a dependent clause that shows the relationship of time, place, condition, or exception to the rest of the sentence.

Whether a clause is independent or dependent, always juxtapose (so you can highlight in pink) its key elements, the Subject and Verb; remember, the goal is lots of pink and no yellow!

Recall the sidebar discussion on the previous page regarding dependent clauses! Don't be discouraged if this still feels awkward.

dependent clauses begin with a subordinating conjunction in front of the subject and verb; common subordinating conjunctions include:

after	although	as	as if	because
before	how	if	since	so that
that	then	though	unless	until
when	whenever	where	whereas	whether
which	while	who	whoever	why
yet				

She submitted her proposal [*before she left the office*].

[*When we saw her*], she was typing furiously.

[*Although I had seen the movie,*] I was eager to go again.

Note that each italicized dependent clause contains both a subject and verb; again, we differentiate phrase and clause solely by the absence (in a phrase) or the presence (in a clause) of both subject and verb. Note also that if we take the subordinating conjunction away, we have an independent clause. Finally, the italicized dependent clause forms the infamous fragment sentence if we do not attach it to the independent clause:

before she left the office—okay, what?

*When **we saw** her*—what happened?

*Although **I had seen** the movie*—so, what?

Three Types of Sentence Construction

Writers classify complete sentences as either **Simple**, **Compound**, or **Complex**. The classification suggests nothing about the thought content of the sentence; rather, it refers to the grammatical constructions used for that particular group of words.

Why do we need to be aware of sentence style? **Reader Comfort!** Frequently a writer can salvage a paragraph that sounds rough just by altering or revising the style of a few sentences rather than rewriting the whole paragraph. If you find five consecutive sentences you wrote in the same style, merely revise sentences two and four to a different style; now, no consecutive sentences bear the same label and the paragraph feels more comfortable to the reader. The paragraph commands more attention because it does not lull or bore the reader.

In the business setting, the **S**imple sentence proves most popular because it expresses one complete

Recall our basic editing premise:

The content is fine, but the presentation strengthens if the writer attends to a few elements that increase clarity and comfort. So far we have used two colors to distinguish strength (pink) and weakness (yellow).

Labeling sentence types:

Use the first letter of the word for each style, and the **x** or **d** at the end for **C**omple**x** and **C**ompoun**d**; if you use plain C or Cp, we will not know what you are referencing. All initial letters are capitalized because the label refers to sentence type, not content.

Thank goodness this is not a grammar book per se; this book puts basic grammar in action to yield powerful business sentences.

thought. The **C**omple**x** sentence is a close second because, as we'll illustrate below, it provides the stage to introduce the main point or to dilute bad news. The **C**ompoun**d** sentence occurs least frequently because business writers usually prefer to present each main idea in a free-standing sentence; nevertheless, the **Cd** sentence plays an important role in sentence construction variety and Reader Comfort.

Strive for sentence construction variety to keep the reader interested. However, you are not looking for an even distribution using the three styles; instead, you just want to monitor that you vary sentence construction.

Understand that our study of sentence classification is quite cursory, by design. Business writers have no need to study sentence construction as grammarians would; instead, we strive to understand clause and phrase well enough to make intelligent choices about the actor/grammatical subject in any sentence we write. Business writers must be sensitive to the impact that subject selection has on Reader Comfort, which relates directly to reader retention.

If you feel comfortable with sentence construction variety, merely skim the next half-chapter; it provides a more detailed discussion of the three basic sentence styles, **S**imple, **C**ompound, and **C**omple**x**. After you skim the material, take a break and rev yourself up for Chapter 3's fascinating discussion of the most important four-letter concept in writing.

If you feel dazed and confused about sentence styles, don't worry; just go to the next page and get comfortable for a friendly discussion of the particulars. Then we'll go on to Chapter 3.

Chapter 2.5—S, Cd, & Cx Sentences

Simple:

A Simple (**S**) sentence contains one independent clause (therefore *one set* of subject and verb) and an unlimited number of phrases. A Simple sentence expresses one complete thought.

<u>She</u> <u>went</u> home (after the meeting). (S)

Here the writer juxtaposed the S/V, and included a prep phrase telling time.

<u>I</u> <u>drove</u> (to the store) (after dinner). (S)

This sentence presents one juxtaposed subject and verb, and two prep phrases, one that tells location and one that tells time.

(Before calling the taxi), <u>I</u> <u>organized</u> the materials (for my presentation). (S)

This Simple sentence begins with a prep phrase establishing time, tells *who did what*, and ends with a prep phrase that presents the relationship between all of the above.

<u>Learning</u> to do something well <u>takes</u> willingness to practice (coupled with good instruction and coaching). (S)

Length is no clue to sentence type. A Simple sentence can be quite long, or very short. If a sentence has only one set of subject and verb, it is a Simple sentence.

Remember, our goal is to juxtapose the subject and verb, and highlight them in pink. If something other than a prep phrase separates subject and verb, underline that interrupter in yellow.

Notice the absence of pink in this sentence. The *who* in *who does what* is vague; the subject requires explanation and definition. Still, the sentence is Simple because it offers only one set of subject and verb.

Compound:

A Compound (**Cd**) sentence contains two or more independent clauses (therefore 2 or more sets of S/V) joined by **coordinating conjunctions**; the writer must present a complete independent clause on each side of the coordinating conjunction. The coordinating conjunctions include **and, but, or, nor.** The semicolon also serves as a coordinating conjunction for purposes of identifying a Compound sentence. In a Compound sentence, each independent clause has equal value; the writer suggests no priority with the placement of the clauses:

> **She went home (after the meeting) and she studied her notes, but she felt unprepared (for her presentation). (Cd)**

All three of these independent clauses have equal value or importance. The prep phrases function well

So, for, yet

were classified as coordinating conjunctions in the past, but newer grammar texts exclude them. Now, grammarians classify *so, for,* and *yet* as subordinating conjunctions (to be used with dependent clauses).

The semicolon:

The semicolon provides a **wonderful** option, yet it is the most abused piece of punctuation we have. The semicolon functions just like a period, or any other coordinating conjunction; it joins two complete thoughts. Its advantage is that it indicates a close relationship between the two clauses, such as cause and effect, action and reaction, or request and response. Semicolons work very well with transition words. Study these examples:

It rained all night; consequently, the driveway flooded.

I requested $2000 for this project; unfortunately, I received only $1500.

What energy! An opportunity this writer could not resist...

to establish relationships, and they do not interfere with S/V juxtaposing.

With a semicolon this sentence reads:

She <u>went</u> home (after the meeting) and she <u>studied</u> her notes; nevertheless, <u>she</u> <u>felt</u> unprepared (for her presentation). (Cd)

The semicolon functions as a period (the reader draws a full breath), but it shows the reader that the ideas relate very closely. Only the reader knows that the writer used a semicolon; if the recipient read this sentence aloud in a meeting, the listeners would assume the writer had used a period between these thoughts. Therein lies the richness of the semicolon; it communicates to the reader a close relationship between independent thoughts. As mentioned in the sidebar note, the semicolon is misunderstood and therefore misused. Don't be afraid of the semicolon; use it to full advantage!

Most <u>people</u> <u>believe</u> in regular exercise, but <u>few</u> <u>put forth</u> the effort. (Cd)

In this Compound sentence we have two complete thoughts joined by the coordinating conjunction *but* to illustrate their relationship. Both thoughts carry equal weight (no pun intended) in a Cd sentence. Note the pink, the S/V juxtaposition.

> **<u>John and Paul</u> <u>presented</u> the program and <u>distributed</u> handouts to assist the listeners. (S!)**

On first blush you might want to label this sentence Compound because it has two subjects and two verbs. However, note how they function. When you ask, *what's the action here?*, the answer is **presented** and **distributed**; then you ask, *who did that?* and the answer is **John and Paul.** Whenever a sentence has what appears to be a coordinating conjunction (**and, but, or, nor**), circle that word and ask yourself if you have a complete sentence on both sides of the circled word. This sentence does not pass that test; **John** is not a complete sentence, nor is **distributed handouts to assist the listeners.**

Complex

A Complex (**Cx**) sentence contains one independent clause and one or more dependent clauses. Usually, writers use Complex sentences to suggest a priority in their thinking; the main clause presents the main idea, and the dependent clause or clauses present the

Be careful here! Remember, *everything* depends on subject and verb!

If we had a subject on the other side of the *and*, we would have a **Cd** sentence:
<u>John and Paul</u> <u>presented</u> the program and <u>they</u> <u>distributed</u> handouts to assist the listeners. (**Cd**)

No rules exist to dictate which clause writers should present first. That's the writer's decision.

less significant information. Further, business writers are well advised to realize that speed readers skim dependent clauses. Therefore, writers might unintentionally sabotage their message if they put important information in a clause that some readers virtually skip.

[Although she did her homework,]
she performed poorly (at the interview). (Cx)

The main idea is that she did poorly at the interview; the lesser idea is that she had prepared. Realize that the writer could flip the clauses to begin the sentence with the independent clause:

She performed poorly at the interview
[although she did her homework]. [Cx]

Notice that with this presentation no comma separates the clauses. This very easy editing maneuver changes the pace of a paragraph, especially if you have a tendency to construct your **Cx** sentences in one particular fashion. Acting as editor, you can switch one or two dependent clauses and realize significant impact on the tone or emphasis of a paragraph. The same principle applies to each of the following sentences:

[When <u>supply</u> <u>is</u> high], <u>value</u> <u>is</u> low. (Cx)

[As <u>Richard</u> <u>walked</u> into the stadium] [before the <u>game</u> <u>began,</u>] the <u>fans</u> <u>stood</u> and <u>applauded</u>. (Cx)

In the second sentence the writer uses two dependent clauses and one independent clause. Even so, the independent clause could come first. Or, for added variety, the writer might present the information like this:

[Before the <u>game</u> <u>began</u>,] the <u>fans</u> <u>stood</u> and <u>applauded</u> [as <u>Richard</u> <u>walked</u> into the stadium.] (Cx)

The point is that writers have great latitude when they realize and then utilize the flexibility of Complex sentences.

<u>I</u> <u>will see</u> you [before <u>I</u> <u>leave</u>]. (Cx)

Let's review the critical difference between phrase and clause using the word *before*. In the last sentence above, **before** is a subordinating conjunction introducing the dependent clause **before I leave**; this

---

Either way, this short sentence is Complex. Reader Comfort determines whether the writer puts the dependent or the independent clause first.

Go for the gusto!

Take full advantage of **S**, **Cd**, **Cx** sentence variety, and placement of clauses in a **Cx** sentence. These editing techniques involve very little revising yet increase Reader Comfort tremendously.

-*ing* words:

Only under two conditions do -*ing* words function as verbs: when a child is about two years old and says, "I going now," or when you have had one too many. Parents rarely tell the child that -*ing* words are not verbs unless they have an auxiliary verb accompanying them. If one of your adult friends told you, "I going now," no doubt you would tell that person to give you his/her keys.

dependent clause makes the sentence Complex. If the writer had chosen to say *before leaving, before* would be a preposition introducing a prep phrase. Then the sentence would be classified as Simple with one independent clause and a prep phrase. Remember, -*ing* words are not verbs unless they have auxiliary verbs with them—*are leaving, am leaving*, etc.

To review, the only difference between these groups of words (clause or phrase) is the presence or absence of subject and verb. What functions as a subordinating conjunction (*before*) in a Complex sentence becomes a preposition (*before*) in a Simple sentence, depending on the presence or absence of subject and verb. Remember, **everything depends on subject and verb!**

Energetic business writers care about sentence construction; the knowledge enables them to write interesting correspondence that inspires the reader. Good sentence variety helps to insure Reader Comfort. When the writer maintains Reader Comfort, the reader is much more likely to respond in the fashion desired by the writer; the reader feels confident that the writer understands the reader's situation and will act appropriately.

Looking at the three sentence construction styles together, consider this. **Simple** does not imply stupid/simplistic; rather, it equates with a simple element in chemistry—only one. A Simple sentence includes only one independent clause.

A **Compound** sentence is two or more **S** sentences (i.e., independent clauses) joined, but suggesting no priority; the reader gleans no clue as to the writer's preference/bias.

A **Complex** sentence presents one independent clause and one or more dependent clauses; with a **Cx** sentence, careful writers hint at their priority and therefore never should put important information in the dependent clause. Just as with prep phrases, speed readers skip/skim dependent clauses. Complex sentences afford great flexibility with the placement of the dependent clause; you can change the pace of a paragraph just by moving a dependent clause, as illustrated below:

I <u>will see</u> you [before <u>I leave</u>].

The independent clause comes first, so the writer includes no comma.

Note that the writer stayed in the pink in each clause!

Before I leave, I will see you.

When the dependent clause comes first, a comma separates it from the independent clause.

Dependent clauses make fine transition devices and "stage setters" for the independent clause that follows. Frequently, writers use dependent clauses to build anticipation or to create interest. Some writers use dependent clauses to present bad or unwelcome news, and then negate or dilute or soften that news as illustrated in the following independent clause(s):

> **[Although we cannot meet your requested schedule,] our staff promises to begin work by the first of March, and we will complete the project within three weeks.**

No doubt the recipient did not want to hear the opening thought; hence, the writer presented that idea in a dependent clause and then quickly offered better news in two consecutive independent clauses.

So far so good? Business writers write to convey information, to get results, or to persuade the reader to take a particular course of action. For maximum Reader Comfort, every sentence must tell *who does*

Appendix B

provides additional practice identifying sentence construction types.

The two independent clauses make this sentence CxCd; note that the Cx element comes first (the dependent clause followed by the independent clause). Then the writer included another independent clause so we have a Cd structure; combined, this yields a CxCd sentence.

Juxtapose:

to position side by side; we strive to do this to avoid confusing readers as they figure out the actor and action in each sentence.

what. You insure comfort and clarity when you juxtapose subject and verb, the most important sentence elements. Chapter 3 focuses on the verb, the **did** of *Who did what?*, and introduces two new pens to the colorful VanWrite Method.

Chapter **3**

Verb--An important four-letter word:

This chapter will change the way you write from this day forward! We will study the weakness inherent in the American verbs of choice--*is, are, was, were*--and demonstrate how to edit them quickly. You will be amazed at the difference this VanWrite concept makes in your writing, and in your thinking.

The Green and Orange of Writing
Paint a Clear Word Picture with Verbs

In the last chapter we studied the importance of juxtaposing subject and verb for maximum Reader Comfort. In addition, we examined the critical difference that subject choice makes. Verb choice plays an equally important role in sentence clarity; this chapter discusses verbs, and explains how verb selection either enlivens or deadens a sentence.

Whenever anyone asks me what I consider the greatest problem with business writing, I reply, "Weak verbs!" Beyond a doubt, weak verbs contribute mightily to the wordiness and confusion found in so many documents. When we write, we concentrate on content and message rather than verb choice. Unfortunately, weak verbs detract from the message we want to send. Think of verbs as the body language of writing. You don't want to come across as static or boring—you want your writing to reflect vitality and vigor. You achieve this vitality when you choose strong verbs.

As creatures of habit and least resistance, we rely on the verbs that come to mind most easily, the **to be** verbs. While these verbs are short, monosyllabic words themselves, they require many other words to qualify, specify, define, or explain them in your sentences.

In any sentence, the verb expresses action, condition, or state of being. Actually, the verb provides the most important part of the sentence; if writers handle the verb structure wisely, they write powerful, grammatically correct sentences. We frequently over-use the verbs *to be*, *to do*, and *to have*. These verbs fill many needs, but we tend to rely on them too heavily because of our familiarity with them. Writers should reduce the use of the following forms of *be*, *have*, and *do* either as main verbs or auxiliary verbs:

TO BE		TO HAVE	TO DO
is	*were*	*has*	*do*
am	*be*	*have*	*does*
are	*being*	*had*	*did*
was	*been*		

In addition, the following verbs bore readers:

shall	*will*	*should*	*would*
may	*might*	*must*	*can*
could			

VanWrite recommends

controlling the number of *to be* verbs in any sentence, not eliminating them totally. When you control or monitor your verbs, you control your message and its reception.

Remember

the expressions "auxiliary verb" or "helping verb"? These verbs are intended to help the main verb to express tense, mood, or passive voice. Sometimes, they only help word count! If you choose a strong verb in active voice initially, you have no need for auxiliary verbs. We use these auxiliary verbs only when we express conditional situations: *I should have worked faster today* ... More on this later.

In my seminars I meet people who memorized the *to be* verbs in elementary school, but they don't recall why. I suggest that you learn to recognize these (boring) verbs so you avoid them in your business writing.

Occasionally, people refer to these verbs as the *static* verbs, as opposed to *action* verbs. *To be* verbs promote or convey no action.

These static and/or passive verbs lull readers and occasionally allow ambiguity in your writing. Overuse of any of the above verbs leads to lackluster prose.

The **to be** verbs don't do anything other than tell us *state of being* or existence. Occasionally verbs like **is, am, are, was**, and **were** make the most economical statements. If I say to you, "Today is Wednesday," that's more straightforward than to say, "Today, arriving after yesterday, appears in our life as Wednesday." You'd say, "Get a life!" The second version uses far too many words to state only what *is*; *today is* Wednesday and it will remain Wednesday until midnight. The concept of "Wednesday" involves no perceptible action; rather, it is a state of being.

In certain sentences, **to be** provides the most credible verb; study the following examples.

I have a headache. vs. A headache dwells in my head.

The first communicates more clearly and quickly than the second. If I tell you, "He has the flu," or "We are tired," those are states of being, so in those instances the state of being verbs work well. However, in business we write about *state of being* quite infrequently. Instead, we write to get action, or to increase our client's confidence in us. We write to promote.

Infinitive...

another word out of the past! An infinitive is a verb form that is not assigned to or associated with the grammatical subject of the sentence; an infinitive includes the word *to* and the verb--*to run, to talk, to write*. The infinitive never functions as the verb of the sentence. For example, in the sentence, *I expect to write the report today*, the verb is *expect*, the subject is *I*, and the infinitive is *to write*.

How do you distinguish an infinitive from a prep phrase? They both begin with *to*. Not a problem! An infinitive offers an action word after *to* as stated above. When *to* functions as a preposition, an article (*a, an, the*) and/or a noun or pronoun follow *to*: *to the store, to the car; to him*.

Is *There* a subject word?

Were you tempted to say **There**? Many people think *There* is the subject in sentences that begin with *There*,

We write to create a vision or an image in our reader's mind. Strong verbs paint word pictures that enable us to do this, and do it efficiently. Therefore, if you deliberately control your use of **to be** verbs, you strengthen your business correspondence.

In the verb chart presented earlier, the infinitives **to have** and **to do** and the other nine verb words form our helping/auxiliary verb expressions. "I *should have gone* ...", "I *might have been* ...", those are the verbs that we use to make auxiliary verb constructions; they don't do much to promote action. Writers use these verbs only when they need to express a conditional situation, or something that is contrary to fact.

Look at this sentence:

There are bookcases on both sides of the fireplace.

Using the approach we began in Chapter 2, what is the action or state of being here, i.e., the verb? The (boring) verb is **are**. To identify the subject, who or what **are**? **bookcases are**. Where **are** the **bookcases**? **(on both sides) (of the fireplace.)** We need two prep phrases to present all the information about location.

but this is never the case. Try to avoid beginning sentences with *There*. At the beginning of a sentence the adverb **There** is a dead word that begs for a boring verb! Think about the verb after *There*--There *is*, There *are*, There *was*, There *were* ... lifeless and useless!

To lower the word count

from nine to four represents a 65% reduction. Yes! Less is more!

Using the VanWrite question *who does what?*, put the subject word at the beginning of the sentence and use a verb that conveys some action or builds an image. **Bookcases** ... do what? If the primo strong verb does not come to mind quickly, go to your thesaurus and look up synonyms for verbs such as *border, surround, outline, frame,* words that *suggest* what the bookcases do:

> **Bookcases *border* the fireplace (on both sides).**

> **Bookcases *surround* the fireplace (on the left and the right).**

If you look for a synonym for **are**, the thesaurus limits you to the **to be** loop. The verbs we used to enter the thesaurus describe the situation much better than (boring) **are** does, but they still require at least one prep phrase to be specific.

The ideal verb in this situation is *flank* because *flank* means "on both sides." If you say,

> **Bookcases flank the fireplace.**

you express in four words what took nine words when the verb reflected no strength!

Green--

the color of money, the environment, go at traffic lights, hills in Spring, everything good in life!

We will practice this VanWrite color code throughout the book.

Orange--

the color of Halloween and other scary concepts like weak business communication.

Research suggests

that 80% of us are visual learners and thinkers, evidenced by familiar expressions such as _I see what you mean,_ and _Do you get the picture?_ If your writing helps the reader visualize your message, you will communicate more clearly. Write to draw word pictures for the reader.

Here we need to introduce two new colors, green and orange. When you have a strong verb, circle it in **green**. In an ideal sentence, the subject and verb appear juxtaposed and highlighted in pink. Hence, we circle the strong verb in **green** because the colors bleed if we impose them on top of each other. If your verb is weak, put an **orange** check above it. In our example prior to editing, _are_ merits an **orange** check. When you read through your documents for verb strength, you want to see at least 70% of your verbs in **green** circles.

Weak verbs always require a great deal of support from other parts of the sentence. Our much shorter, revised sentence clearly reveals _who does what_, and it includes no prep phrases, one of the constructions that speed readers skim or skip. Contrast the revision with the original --

> ✓
> **There <u>are bookcases</u> (on both sides) (of the fireplace).**

and realize that the hurried reader focuses on subject and verb and pays little attention to anything else in

Word Choice

In spoken language, weak verbs are more acceptable because the speaker uses gestures, inflection, eye contact, and overall body language. In writing, word choice provides our only shot!

the sentence. Net result? *Bookcases are!* All the news *about* the bookcases goes virtually unnoticed.

Writers need to use strong verbs to insure that their readers will remember the message the next day, or a week later. In our example, you will remember where the bookcases are because when you read the sentence the first time, you visualized the setting immediately; that mental picture made a "take" in your mind. If someone calls you the next day and asks the location of the bookcases in that room, you'd reply that they are on either side of the fireplace, or they frame the fireplace on the left and right, or they *flank* the fireplace. Whether or not you use the exact verb you read is unimportant; what matters is that you recall the message because the writer used a precise, strong, visual word.

Here's another sentence construction we see frequently:

The walls are covered with wallpaper.

For this sentence you might say on first glance that we are in good shape because the subject and verb are juxtaposed. True, but what is the action/state of being? <u>are covered</u>, a weak verb construction. Who

Passive verb/Passive voice

The subject receives the action of the verb, rather than performing that action:

The report was presented by Tom. ✓

(The report did nothing! Tom is the active party here, but he is hidden in a prep phrase rather than being presented in subject position.) Passive voice uses some form of *to be* with the action word.

Active verb/Active voice:

The subject performs the action identified by the verb:

Tom presented the report.

Active voice answers the question, *Who did what?* The reader experiences no confusion, and word count diminishes favorably.

or what are covered? <u>walls</u> <u>are covered</u>. However, remember that we always want to know who does what in every sentence we examine.

In the example sentence above, the word in subject position isn't really the actor; **walls** *receive* the action. In short, we have a *passive verb*. When we say **The walls are covered**, the only thing the walls did was stand there and let something happen to them. Look in the prep phrase for a better subject/actor. **Wallpaper** is not an actor with a heartbeat nor can it make decisions on its own; it's another *thing*, an inanimate object. However, what does wallpaper *do?* It *covers* walls! *Covers* is a strong, *active verb*.

A much stronger, more logical sentence reads:

Wallpaper covers the walls.

This revision yields a more reasonable subject/actor, it maintains subject-verb juxtapositioning, and it eliminates both the prep phrase and the boring verb. When you question *who does what?* you force a strong subject/actor capable of action, and a strong active verb. In addition, you paint a clear picture. Reader Comfort and understanding soar once again!

Generally, when you edit for verbs you shorten the sentence by taking out unnecessary words—the dead-

Remember, verbs function as the body language of writing. Forget the old idea that more words make a better document. Active voice represents writing fitness.

Weak verbs promote wordy sentences; strong verbs energize and trim business writing.

wood. For instance, how would you make the following a more powerful sentence?

I am the owner (of twenty-five acres) (of land).

Is it necessary to announce that you are the owner? No! Use a verb that expresses that concept as an action and ignore your state of being. Also, we only need to specify *of land* if the reader is in danger of thinking you own a water ski lake or a lagoon! Realize the trap the writer set with the use of a weak verb. To reiterate: weak verbs require lots of support from other areas of the sentence; hence, the writer needed two prep phrases to express what he owns. A much stronger revision reads:

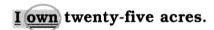

I own twenty-five acres.

This sentence juxtaposes a strong actor with a strong action, it tells *who does what*, and it eliminates all prep phrases. (Beautiful colors, too!)

Again, business writing becomes much clearer and more vital when you ***reduce*** the use of the verbs *to be, to have* and *to do*. We cannot eliminate their use, nor is it desirable to do so. Occasionally in your professional life you need to use weak verbs or vague verbs because you are unsure of an event's outcome, or you do not know who the specific actor will be, or you want to protect somebody.

However, you need to avoid weak, lifeless verbs anytime you intend to be direct, commanding, and concise. For instance, look at this example:

> ✓
> All **information will be provided** Thursday.

On first blush that's a fine sentence, and certainly grammatically correct; nevertheless, with closer study you realize that it does not convey *who does what*. The sentence lacks a believable actor in subject position. Recall the discussion in Chapter 2 about the importance of an identified actor. Without that actor, the reader feels dissatisfied.

Now, you might say you are not going to announce the *who* because you don't know yet who's doing the presentation on Thursday; in that case, fine, hide behind a weak presentation to buy more time to work out the details. On the other hand, if you do know who the actor will be, and it's okay to announce, then say,

> Our **department plans** ..., or

> The **ABC team intends** to provide all information on Thursday.

Choosing Actors

The actor need not be an individual; you may choose a group and any of the nouns that describe that group—*our team, this office, our department, we, our consultants, the managers, the analysts*—the list goes on. Hide behind the corporate veil if you desire, but draft an actor (i.e., choose a subject) capable of acting. Give your readers the human touch!

Where do you find strong business verbs?

Appendix C presents an abbreviated list of strong verbs; cruise the list for inspiration. Note that the offerings are regular words rather than unnatural or academic.

Use a strong verb and provide an actor—tell your readers *who does what!* Comfort your readers and communicate with them.

Another difficult verb situation occurs when we write in the future tense. Some documents sound like they are full of hollow promises but no concrete action when every sentence includes **will** in the verb structure: "We will do this" and "We will do that." The reader may think that currently you do very little, but you might swing into action at some later date.

Try this approach to reduce the use of **will** when you write about the future. Project yourself or your organization to that time and write as though it is the present. Assume a customer or client asks how you will perform a particular task or function for them. In your proposal you sound more confident and experienced if you make the future your present tense; for example,

> **Every time we do X, we always purchase and install the necessary equipment. Then we train staff and remain available to troubleshoot during the trial period.**

Realize also that every time you use **will** you're forming a verbal contract and a potential noose from

The color scheme indicates the strength.

Note that all the verbs paint green, suggesting vigor, and each sentence tells *who does what.* The reader feels very comfortable.

which you could dangle at a later time. You don't want to do that!

Of course, in many contracts, **will** and **shall** carry legal implications necessary for the contract to have meaning and clout. Frequently, staff writers are not at liberty to alter legal phrasing. Whenever possible, however, use a present tense verb such as *expect, plan, intend, anticipate,* or *project,* frequently coupled with an infinitive. For instance:

> **We intend to complete this project June 30.**

> **We anticipate a June 30 completion date.**

> **We plan to submit our final budget May 1.**

These sentences present no auxiliary or helping verbs.

Regarding verbs, yet another writing dilemma occurs when we have to write about ourselves or others; we experience difficulty presenting the information without using static verbs. Ironically, in the business setting usually we write about people to promote them or honor them or recognize them for their accomplishments. Sadly, we use verbs that make the article or memo read flat precisely when we need vitality:

(At XYZ Corp.) John was responsible (for payroll complaints).

Why tell the reader he was *responsible?* Hopefully, that goes without saying. *Show* the reader! The first prep phrase is fine because it establishes location, one of the primary functions of prep phrases; however,the second prep phrase hides the most important news! Yet, as we discussed above, when writers use weak verbs, they have to use several other words to support that verb. A much more commanding sentence states:

(At XYZ Corp.) John resolved payroll complaints.

This revision makes the actor pro-active due to verb choice, and it eliminates the last prep phrase.

To bring your prose to life, and to give your documents the tone you want, use strong verbs. Write about yourself and others in present tense rather than past; when you use present tense verbs you avoid helping/auxiliary verbs, those words that take up space but do little to advance your message.

Regarding personnel, the most unenviable business writing situation occurs when you need to write a

Chapters 5 and 6 provide lively editing discussions of business sentences. The simple VanWrite Method revolves around the same question for every sentence: *Who does/did what?* A strong actor performing a strong action yields a strong sentence! Don't worry-- this process becomes easier with practice.

Scary verb colors,

and oh-so-negative. . . cruel!

letter of reprimand regarding an employee's behavior or performance. Your first draft might include sentences like:

> ✓
> **You must not leave work early without checking out formally.**

> ✓
> **You can't expect your colleagues to be responsible for your problems.**

> ✓   ✓
> **You will be terminated if you do not change these behaviors.**

Two major problems exist with such phrasing. First, the recipient feels very attacked because of all the **You** statements; the employee becomes very defensive. Consequently he/she puts energy into rebuttal rather than learning how to conform to the office culture. The employee ignores the message and gets caught up in the presentation and tone.

Secondly, the writer sounds like Cinderella's wicked stepmother beating up on the employee. To avoid conflicts such as these, draft the "higher authority" or corporate structure as actor in your sentences and use your letter as a reminder of protocol:

Department policy requires all employees to check out formally if **they need** to leave work early.

Our **contract demands** that each **employee takes** two breaks a day.

Our **contract makes** no provisions for banking break time to be used later at the employee's discretion.

Put the authority where it belongs, with the employer and/or the organization.

The writer changed the actor from the employee under criticism to the employer who makes policy; this eliminated the attack posture from the letter. Note, too, that these revisions also include strong, present tense (green) verbs that support the employer.

In all writing efforts, be sure to tell the reader what you want. That seems so obvious! Yet when writers riddle their writing with negatives, they avoid making a straightforward statement that shows what they

Cinderella's stepmother does not work in *this* office!

The writer feels justified and more objective, and the recipient feels coached rather than attacked.

really want. Study the differences in these two statements:

Don't put the mail on the front desk. vs.

Put the mail in the in-basket.

The first sentence does not provide a clear directive. The employee is likely to put the mail in several places rather than in the in-basket. The second sentence specifically tells the employee what to do. Anytime you remove a negative from your writing, you write a much more direct statement. Positive statements instruct! Reader Comfort prevails.

This same lack of specificity occurs when you use the passive voice. The reader is not motivated to action because the writer hides the directive so well:

Enclosed is a graph for your review.

Most readers respond to such a sentence with something like, "OK, fine..." If the writer tells the reader what to do with the enclosure, the reader will respond accordingly:

Please review the enclosed graph to understand our position.

So what is the subject?

Good question. In this revised sentence, the action (verb) is *review*; then ask, "Who or what *review* ...?" The answer is **you!** In English, the only implied subject is "you understood."

Remember "you understood?" If I look at you and say, "Answer the phone," the verb is *answer*, and the subject is *you*. It is "understood" or "implied." Perhaps you recall this as the *command form*.

How's your pulse and respiration at this point? Do you need a cool down? With just a little practice you will use these colors to resolve your writing problems rather than to increase your heartbeat, I promise!

Now the reader knows what to do and why! The reader is much more motivated to invest a few minutes reviewing the graph because the writer explained the benefit of doing so. This practice seems so obvious, but when writers work under pressure, they frequently ignore the obvious because *they* know what they mean or intend to communicate.

Let's **pause** here and **review** what we know about the VanWrite Method. Whenever you review a document, whether it is your own or one written by someone else, focus on any sections that lack Reader Comfort. In your quest to remedy the weakness(es), begin your analysis by identifying the subject and verb in each sentence. First, ask yourself what the action or state of being is in the sentence; this reveals the verb, which you <u>underline twice</u>. Then, ask who or what does that action; this uncovers the subject (actor), which you <u>underline once</u>. Hopefully these two elements (subject and verb) are juxtaposed (side by side), so you highlight them in pink. If you find a prep phrase between the subject and verb, highlight that in yellow to indicate the potential for reader confusion. Next, look at the verbs. If they are strong, circle them in green. If they are weak, put orange checks above them. You will find that the coloring

Remember, frequently yellow
means the subject is weak
or vague and needs to be qualified: try to draft a strong actor
hidden somewhere else in the
sentence.

Glaring colors!

Low Reader Comfort.
Who did what?

Much better colors!

This sentence tells *who did
what.*

Don't

make a career out of changing
verbs! Be reasonable about
this--choose the verbs that fix
rather easily. Take comfort in

goes quickly, and the colors immediately indicate
the problems.

After you color with these four pens, start your
target editing. I recommend that you try to eliminate
all yellow because every time the subject and verb
split, the reader has an opportunity to become confused, or at least to feel uncomfortable. Yellow makes
the reader work too hard to follow your thinking.
Most readers will not spend energy trying to plow
through the document.

Yellow and orange seem to have an affinity for one
another. Frequently, when you edit the yellow you
simultaneously resolve the orange. Note this sentence and its revision:

> **The <u>plants</u> (for the waiting room) <u>were pur-
> chased</u> (by my associate).** ✓

> **My <u>associate</u> (purchased) the plants (for the
> waiting room).**

How many of the orange checks should you try to
abolish? Aim for about 60% of them; assuming you
had a fair amount of green circles (strong verbs) initially, 60% fewer weak verbs insures a strong, clear,
commanding document.

the idea that every verb edit improves your document and makes your writing stronger than the competition's!

Remember, weak verbs result in weak writing, which reflects weak thinking.

If you manage others, you review their writing daily. When you receive a document that seems wordy and difficult to understand, paint the rough area(s) and focus on the verbs for a few minutes. If most of the verbs are weak--static, state of being, passive, auxiliary--the writer might not understand the topic. Remember, writers use many extra words to support a weak verb.

If you determine this to be the problem, you have a couple of choices. You could roll up your sleeves and begin editing to include stronger verbs, consequently shortening the sentences. Or, you could give the document back to the author and instruct that person to strengthen the verbs. However, the most productive course of action suggests that you confer with the author and ask, "Do you understand the issues? Can I help you understand our focus for this project?"

You will unearth and resolve the problem quickly when you realize that the weak verbs suggest the writer's discomfort with the task. Verbs play a vital role in writing's precision and Reader Comfort; comprehending this, you no longer stare at a document, knowing there's something wrong but not being sure what it is. The verbs provide a strong signal that a real gap may exist in the writer's understanding. Of course, this applies to your own writing, too! Step back and look at the colors; then proceed accordingly.

Ideal business colors:

So far what is the ideal color scheme to insure clarity? Pink and green! In business writing avoid the obnoxious yellow and orange.

An additional benefit comes with color coding another writer's document; coloring is unemotional. When you return a painted document to the writer, you haven't blasted that person about writing style or thinking. Instead, you show the writer what needs to be addressed to increase Reader Comfort.

The seemingly boring verbs do have (!) a place in our writing; however, let's severely limit that place. Limit it to:

- those discussions of state of being--very few;

- those times when you need to waffle because you do not want to, or cannot, be straightforward-- hopefully very few, too!

- those discussions of conditional situations--If I had worked harder I would have finished earlier.

The verb provides the vitality and energy of your sentence, the "go" power; make sure you use green verbs that create the image you want to present, to paint the clear word picture. Your attention to verb choice will strengthen your writing more than any other single concept. Most writers use weak, lazy verbs. Edit your writing to include verbs with vigor! Of course, be sure to juxtapose the active verb with a lively or believable actor. Empower your thinking to target edit!

4

Chapter

Technical writing
includes instructions, job speci-
fications, manuals, and
documentation.

Narrative writing
includes all other prose (non-
poetry).

The Blue and Purple of Writing
Smooth and Easy Reading

Transitions

Every piece of writing needs transitional words and phrases to increase coherence and Reader Comfort. Quickly, common transitions include *therefore, however, likewise, in addition, then,* and *next*; we discuss these and several others later in the chapter. Transitions help the reader move from one point to another and prevent the text from sounding disjointed or choppy.

No formula exists prescribing the number of transitions to include in a particular paragraph. Use your judgment, based on your reader's familiarity with your topic. Generally, the more technical documents require a greater number of transitions because the reader depends on consecutive thoughts to grasp the whole. Conversely, more narrative documents might require fewer transitions because natural transitions result from the sequence of events or the passage of time.

To identify transitions, underline them with your highlighter pen. In concert with pink (S/V

Think of transitions as spices;

for instance, a touch of curry adds interest and definition to a dish. However, if you add too much, you ruin the food. Likewise with transitions--if you use them well, you enhance Reader Comfort, enabling your reader to understand and retain your message; on the other hand, if you overuse transitions, your reader becomes distracted by them.

Why did we stay home? **We felt tired.** The transition allows the writer to combine the thoughts smoothly.

juxtaposed) and green (strong verbs), blue is the third color that insures clarity in every document you write. The following transition words and phrases prove useful in business—and personal—writing. In no way do these lists present all the possible transitions appropriate for each category; instead, they serve as examples only. Generally, business writers use transitions from the four main categories discussed on the following pages.

Cause-and-effect relationships:

consequently	as a result
therefore	immediately
thus	due to this fact
so	

These transitions work especially well after semicolons. The semicolon serves as a visual clue to the reader that what follows the semicolon relates very closely to what preceded it. A semicolon requires a complete sentence on each side. When you use a semicolon, you construct a Compound sentence; in other words, the two individual complete thoughts complement or form one larger idea. Study these examples:

We felt tired all day Saturday; consequently, we stayed home.

Our office (purchased) a new computer system; as a result, we (respond) to customer inquiries much faster.

Cause-and-effect transition words reinforce your message and enable the reader to grasp the relationship easily. Blue represents a very important color for clarity.

Compare and contrast:

likewise	however
similarly	on the other hand
in the same way	nevertheless
in addition	in contrast
on the whole	in spite of

Regarding compare and contrast: beware! Traditionally, *compare* refers to the *similarities*, and *contrast* refers to *differences*. Hence, if I compare two vehicles, I focus on their similarities; both have four wheels on the ground, a stereo, a transmission, a fast engine, etc. If I contrast these same vehicles, I focus on the specific differences—one is four-wheel drive and one is a sports car, one has six doors but the other has only two doors, one has 16" tires while the other has 13" tires.

Curiously, our culture adjusted these meanings to fit particular purposes, and now we see advertisements that read, "Compare our prices. We are lowest." Shouldn't that be impossible? If you compare, you look for the similarities! *Lowest* is a difference, not a comparison. Interesting, you say, but, so?

If a client asks you to *compare* two concepts, what will you do? Will you address only the similarities, or will you include the differences? This question becomes very important in a proposal situation that requires you to be "responsive" at every phase. Get clarification! If you do not, you risk ignoring half of the client's request, OR you risk doing twice as much work as the client wants. Usually, business writers use *compare* to mean compare-and-contrast, but don't bet on this one; clarify the expectation from the beginning.

Note how these transition words impact meaning:

Our department suffered a 9% budget cut; likewise, Personnel absorbed a 4% cut.

Our department suffered a 9% budget cut; in contrast, Personnel took 4% cut.

Also note
the clarity and strength provided by the green verbs.

likewise
indicates that both departments experienced similar setbacks.

in contrast
suggests the differences that the two departments experienced in the cuts.

Time relationships:

after	at this point	currently
finally	first	frequently
later	next	now
soon	then	when

These transitions probably seem the most obvious because they reflect and reinforce the natural order of events. Use these transitions with Reader Comfort foremost on your mind. If your topic is especially technical and the issue is relatively new to your reader, include these each time you change focus. When writing instructions, you will find these transitions very valuable for clarity; they pace the reader and allow the reader to comprehend the text much more easily. Note this mundane example:

Whenever you mow the lawn, you need to follow a particular sequence to guarantee a quality job. First, remove any foreign objects from the lawn so you may proceed without interruption. Then edge the entire perimeter. Next, check the mower to insure it is in good working order and has plenty of gas.

People who hire gardeners do not have to worry about this sequence.

We use transitions for the reader's benefit, for Reader Comfort. Occasionally, as writers we ignore transitions because *we* experience very little difficulty with the order or sequence; we know what we want to say, and we have an internal sense of order regarding the topic. Unfortunately, the reader may not! Let a passage "cool off" before you make the final determination about transitions. In the heat of writing we sometimes experience difficulty anticipating the reader's need for guidance. However, when we reread a passage or a document later, we understand more easily where we need to include transitions.

Examples:

a case in point	for instance
another	to illustrate
such as	besides
furthermore	in addition
for example	perhaps the most
one reason	

These transitions serve to introduce supportive material. Note that several of these transitions actually express the time sequence or priority of an argument or concept as illustrated in the following paragraph:

Regarding *one reason*

Some writers are tempted to write something like, "One reason is because we lack funding." Audiences frown upon this practice. Why? If you use this construction, you create an empty independent clause--One _reason_ _is_ --and all the information falls in a dependent clause. Too wordy, and unnecessarily weak! Instead, write, "One _reason_ _addresses_ lack of funding." In a Simple sentence, this edit juxtaposes a strong verb with the subject.

In addition, we installed new printers. One reason addressed the lack of speed provided by the old printers. Furthermore, we experienced difficulty finding replacement parts. Finally, our production schedule demanded reliable equipment.

The dependent clause serves as another *very* useful transition. Recall that careful writers try to avoid putting major information in dependent clauses; however, the dependent clause is a *wonderful* transition, especially at the beginning of the sentence.

When you leave the office,. . .

As soon as you begin the meeting,. . .

Underline both of these dependent clauses in blue because they function as transitions, moving the focus from one concept to another. Similarly, if you open a sentence with a prep phrase that functions as a transition, underline the phrase.

Transitions play a very significant role in Reader Comfort. When you highlight your writing to visualize its strengths and weaknesses, make sure every document offers a healthy sampling of blue.

Remember, all dependent clauses contain their own subject and verb, elements you no doubt juxtaposed and painted pink and green. (Thank you very much.)

Your choice here depends on how much you like the color blue!

Unity

This section discusses paragraph unity, a very important concept for Reader Comfort. To illustrate the importance of paragraph unity, study the following writing sample and monitor your Reader Comfort level:

When the department manager is asked to make a formal speech, he goes through a stressful period to prepare. First, the requesting party indicates the preferred topic of the speech. Then staff members research the topic. Some staff visit libraries while other staff conduct interviews with people knowledgeable in the subject area. A third group performs a public awareness survey on the issue to determine the issue's volatility. Then the secretary organizes all the material for my manager to review. At this time a call is made to determine the availability of easels, markers, and overhead projectors. Finally, when all the research is completed and organized, staff coaches the manager so that his speech will be

Does this paragraph remind you of writing you read everyday? Plow through—we will edit for comfort.

interesting and informative. The stress always proves to be productive because the manager always delivers a brilliant speech.

As a reader, you probably feel somewhat confused and frustrated by this paragraph, as though you have been jerked around unnecessarily. Paragraph unity refers to the way the specific grammatical subjects relate to the paragraph topic in general. Let's paint this passage to see if we can pinpoint the problem. We begin by underlining the subject and verb in each sentence.

When the <u>department manager</u> <u>is asked</u> to make a formal speech, <u>he</u> <u>goes</u> through a stressful period to prepare. First, the <u>requesting party</u> <u>indicates</u> the preferred topic of the speech. Then <u>staff members</u> <u>research</u> the topic. <u>Staff</u> <u>visit</u> libraries while <u>staff</u> <u>conduct</u> interviews with people knowledgeable in the subject area. A third <u>group</u> <u>performs</u> a public awareness survey on the issue to determine the issue's volatility. Then the <u>secretary</u> <u>organizes</u> all the material for my manager to review. At this time a

Remember

the questions that reveal subject and verb:

What's the action here? = <u>Verb</u>

Who is doing it? = <u>Subject</u>

is asked includes the verb and its helping verb.

VanWrite Color Code:

To review—
(S = subject, V = verb)
Pink = S/V juxtaposed
Yellow = Prep phrase between
  S/V
Green = Strong verb
Orange = Weak verb
Blue = Transitions

call is made to determine the availability of easels, markers, and overhead projectors. Finally, when all the research is completed and organized, staff coaches the manager so that his speech will be interesting and informative. The stress always proves to be productive because the manager always delivers a brilliant speech.

After you identify the subject(s) and verb(s) in each sentence, uncap your pens and highlight the elements appropriately; the results should look like this:

When the department manager is asked to make a formal speech, he goes through a stressful period to prepare. First, the requesting party indicates the preferred topic of the speech. Then staff members research the topic. Some staff visit libraries while other staff conduct interviews with people knowledgeable in the subject area. A third group performs a public awareness survey on the issue to determine the issue's volatility. Then the secretary organizes all

the material for my manager to review. **At this time** a call **is made** to determine the availability of easels, markers, and overhead projectors. **Finally,** when all the research **is completed** and organized, staff **coaches** the manager so that his speech **will be** interesting and informative. **The** stress **always proves** to be productive because the manager **always** delivers a brilliant speech.

Guess what? This passage paints beautifully; we identify regular subject/verb juxtapositioning--lots of pink, strong green verbs throughout, and a generous dose of transitions--blue. However, the Reader Comfort remains quite low. What's going on here, you ask?

At this point, study the paragraph unity--the relationship between the topic sentence and all the other sentences in the paragraph. In any document, each paragraph's topic sentence should function as a contract with the reader. The topic sentence establishes the reader's expectations, and the remaining sentences serve to support that topic sentence.

In this passage, the topic sentence is

> When the **department manager** **is asked** ✓ to make a formal speech, **he goes** through a stressful period to prepare.

Examine the passage once more, looking at each sentence to determine if the grammatical subject supports the idea in the topic sentence's main clause. The topic sentence actor should act in most of the sentences.

As you begin to evaluate the unity of any paragraph, put a **purple X** above the grammatical subject(s) in the topic sentence; then, throughout the paragraph, continue this practice--put a **purple X** above the grammatical subject *if* it reflects or is a synonym for the subject in the topic sentence.

> When the **department manager** X **is asked** ✓ to make a formal speech, **he goes** X through a stressful period to prepare. First, the **requesting party indicates** the preferred topic of the speech. Then **staff members research** the topic. Some **staff visit** libraries while other **staff conduct** interviews with people knowledgeable in the subject area. A

Unity:

Everything depends on "who's on first" regarding paragraph unity! Writers must pay attention to the words they choose to put in subject position.

As we scan this paragraph for purple X's, we see that in most sentences the subject words have nothing to do with the *department manager* or *he.*

third group performs a public awareness survey on the issue to determine the issue's volatility. Then the secretary organizes all the material for my manager to review. At this time a call is made to determine the availability of easels, markers, and overhead projectors. Finally, when all the research is completed and organized, staff coaches the manager so that his speech will be interesting and informative. The stress always proves to be productive because the manager always delivers a brilliant speech.

As we scan for **purple X**'s, immediately we note their alarmingly scarce occurrence. No wonder this paragraph lacked Reader Comfort! The topic sentence told us that the manager goes through a stressful period when he is asked to make a speech. Apparently the stress incapacitates the man; the rest of the paragraph introduces a cast of thousands who swings into action, no doubt as the manager faints away. Hence, this paragraph lacks unity, or focus, and consequently it lacks coherence. The writer did not focus on the manager at all, so the paragraph is almost incoherent to the reader.

When you evaluate a passage for unity, ask yourself if you told your reader what you promised; did you stay focused, or did you take a side trip and ignore the verbal "contract" you made with the reader? If you find that you did break the contract, that your passage lacks unity, don't despair! You have two choices; just remember, everything depends on subject and verb, and "who's on first." Those choices rest with you.

First, you can restore paragraph unity by changing the topic sentence so it reflects what actually follows. In our example, the new topic sentence might read:

> **[When the department manager is asked to make a formal speech], the entire staff goes through a stressful period to prepare.**

Now it becomes reasonable to meet all these other players--the entire staff, in fact. The reader expects the paragraph to develop the idea of total staff involvement. If you use this technique to repair paragraph unity, make sure that you do not compromise the focus of the document *overall.* Changing the topic sentence works best for single-paragraph memos such as the one we studied here. In a longer document, we assume each paragraph builds on a larger topic or

department manager
is the subject of the dependent clause; *staff* becomes the subject of the independent clause, the most important element of the sentence.

Return to chapter 2.5 to review independent and dependent clauses.

Italics

The italics reveal how the VanWrite Method pivots on target editing rather than wholesale rewriting. The author only had to choose a new actor (subject) and action (verb) in each sentence rather than rewrite the entire sentence.

Review:

Note, too, that when you maintain a strong actor throughout the paragraph, the verbs also reflect strength. Recall that passive and weak verbs result from lousy words in subject

thesis idea expressed in the document's introduction. In such cases, you do not have as much freedom to change an individual topic sentence.

The second solution involves changing the grammatical subject, the actor, in each sentence so the grammatical subject reflects the topic sentence more accurately. Contrast the crossed-out subjects with the new actor in the revision below. The italics indicate the revised wording to achieve paragraph unity and coherence.

When the department manager is asked to make a formal speech, he goes through a stressful period to prepare. First, *he learns from the requesting party* the requesting party indicates the preferred topic of the speech. Then *he asks* staff members to research staff members research the topic. Some staff visit libraries while other staff conduct interviews with people knowledgeable in the subject area. A third group performs a public awareness survey on the issue to determine the issue's volatility. Then *the manager asks* the secretary to organize secretary organizes all the material

position, words that cannot do anything:

A decision was made by the staff.

Boring, dull, weak. Who did what? *Decision* cannot do anything; *decision* results from some human action.

Staff made a decision.

Much better! Real live humans at work!

Better yet:
(how do you "make a decision," with sifted or unsifted flour? Cut to the chase!)

Staff decided to. . .

for ~~my manager to~~ *his* review. At this time *the* manager makes a call ~~call is made~~ to determine the availability of easels, markers, and overhead projectors. Finally, when all the research is completed and organized, ~~staff coaches~~ *the* manager receives *coaching from the staff* so that his speech will be interesting and informative. The stress always proves to be productive because the manager always delivers a brilliant speech.

Now this paragraph reflects unity and coherence; the actor in the topic sentence acts in most of the sentences. In the topic sentence, we put a **purple X** above *he*, the word in subject position in the independent clause. Then we looked for that actor to be the grammatical subject in other sentences in the paragraph. Bingo! That word, or a synonym, functions as subject the majority of the time. What a boost to clarity!

Consider another aspect of paragraph unity. Hard as it is to stomach, *occasionally* you need to use passive verbs in order to maintain paragraph unity! Initially this seems to contradict Chapter 3's discussion of strong verbs, but the larger issue here focuses on Reader Comfort throughout the paragraph. Assume you need to write a paragraph about the trees in City Park and who takes care of them, an example near the beginning of Chapter 2. If the *trees* need to be in subject position in most of the paragraph's sentences, you need to use passive verbs because *trees do not do* anything (except grow and blossom and produce fruit). The actors with the heartbeats play second fiddle to the trees themselves. The paragraph might read as follows:

> **Originally, the <u>trees</u> in City Park <u>were planted</u> by the Lion's Club. After they began to show significant growth, the <u>trees</u> <u>were maintained</u> by the City Parks Department. In the past the <u>trees were pruned</u> by the Garden Club. Currently, the <u>trees are cared for</u> by members of the Senior Center.**

In this example, *trees* appear in subject position throughout the paragraph. If we had put the human actors in subject position, this paragraph would change focus with every sentence; the paragraph would lack unity *and* Reader Comfort. Of course,

When a situation demands a particular focus, occasionally we need to use passive verbs to maintain that focus; the topic is more important than the actor.

In business writing, readers experience most comfort when strong, believable actors act.

Blue and Purple--

represent smooth transitions and frequent subject identification. These are the last two beautiful colors of powerful, clear business writing.

as with the longer example above, the writer could change the topic sentence to read,

Many organizations contribute to the maintenance of the trees in City Park.

Then we would expect to see evidence of the many groups. However, such a switch would detract from the focus on the trees. With any document, the writer must decide which concept to advance as the topic idea. It's your call; just be sure that you are consistent!

Blue and purple insure high Reader Comfort. Structure your writing so that you offer a pleasing amount of each color for smooth and easy reading.

Congratulations! You have met and explored the VanWrite Method and its six clarifying colors. The next three chapters provide examples and exercises (with answers) to reinforce your understanding of the concepts that enable you to target edit.

Target Editing

Chapter 5

VanWrite Premise:

If you are attentive to sentence construction variety, you have a powerful editing tool available; you are able to do a targeted revision rather than a blind rewrite.

To demonstrate the various grammatical elements of each original sentence, I used the editing marks we use throughout the book:

> subject
> verb
> (Prep phrase)
> [dependent clause]
> S/V = subject and verb

Those Amazing Colors of Clarity
See the Full Spectrum

This chapter provides annotated examples of typical business writing *before* and *after* editing with the VanWrite Method. Contrast the color schemes in the original and the edited versions. We always strive for the power colors--pink, blue, and green (girls, boys, and money). In several examples the edits involve changing the sentence construction. Study the weaknesses in each original passage below; then note the suggested edits that increase Reader Comfort.

To increase your comfort as you study this chapter, I devoted a full page to each sample sentence. This provides space for you to practice additional edits and to make notes to yourself. Use this chapter as a workbook to help you comprehend and embrace the VanWrite Method.

Sentences 1-4 illustrate unnecessarily wordy writing; consequently, the writer sounds weak and unfocused:

Avoid **not** whenever possible; if hurried readers miss the **not**, they misunderstand your message completely.

This edit allows the writer to tell the reader exactly what the writing accomplished, and it states the *main message* in the main/independent clause. The reader feels very confident in the writer's ability to deliver. In addition, word count decreased 35%, from 23 words to 15.

1. Our proposal is designed to demonstrate [that we not only have the resources to meet your needs, but we also have the staff.] (Cx)

The reader asks if the writer succeeds or not! Yes, the subject and verb are juxtaposed in the independent clause, but the verb is weak, and the independent clause offers no real news. In addition, the dependent clause contains a confusing **not**. As illustrated below, a more succinct edit puts the *proposal* in the dependent clause, and uses the original infinitive as the main verb; also, this allows the dependent clause to function as a transition. Now the independent clause showcases the writer's strengths, and deletes other unnecessary words:

> **[As our proposal demonstrates,] we have the resources and the staff to meet your needs. (Cx)**

This revision illustrates all the colors of clarity!

Be aware of your use of dependent vs. independent clauses as you present your message. If you begin with a dependent clause, your independent clause will present the "proof"-- *As we proved in Section I, we have the expertise to do this job.* Also, the dependent clause functions as a transition. However, if you begin with an independent clause, you force the "proof" into a dependent clause—*Section I proves that we have the expertise to do this job.* I recommend the first approach—it puts the main news in the main clause.

Remember, a Simple sentence includes only one set of subject and verb, and an unlimited number of phrases.

2. [As we attempted to prove (in Section I,)]. . .

This dependent clause inspires little reader confidence; again, dependent clauses function well as transitions and introductions, but be positive in introductory dependent clauses! Don't tell your audience what you *attempted*; show them the desired results:

As we proved in Section I. . .

Furthermore, originally *Section I* appears in a prep phrase *within* a dependent clause. If you decide to make *Section I* the actor, and to open with an independent clause, the (62% shorter!) edit reads:

Section I proves. . .

If you want to write a Simple sentence, you need to avoid a dependent clause. Your edit might read like this:

Section I proves our ability to do this job. (S)

Frequently the writer only has to look around in a sentence to draft an existing word to a new role—*summary* becomes *summarizes.*

Be lean!

Gone are the days of "more is better"; we live in leaner times!

3. **This letter is intended as a summary (of our brief conversation last week). (S)**

The reader wonders if the letter's intentions were realized! Choose a stronger verb that suggests a stronger purpose; note, too, that the edit eliminates the prep phrase:

This letter summarizes our brief conversation last week. (S)

The edit reduces the word count by 38%, from 13 to 8; why overload the reader? Furthermore, the writer sounds much more confident.

The edit you choose depends
on the sentence style you want;
this Simple sentence opens
with a prep phrase, features
one independent clause, and
ends with a prep phrase. The
Complex sentence opens with
an independent clause, and
puts *attorneys* in a dependent
clause. It's your call, based on
the demand for sentence construction variety.

Observation:

Repeatedly we are told this
is the "Information Age."
Curiously, some business
writers still cling to the
bureaucratic style that
seemingly strives to *hide*
information in a sentence.

4. **Again, from my experience, staff attorneys appear to be concerned primarily (with three things). (S)**

What are "things"? Find a different noun. And "appear"—what does that mean? Not a pro-active verb.

Again, from my experience, staff attorneys focus primarily (on three issues). (S)

or

My experience suggests [that staff attorneys focus primarily (on three issues)]. (CX)

Whether you choose to use a Simple or a Complex sentence depends on the surrounding sentences, and your choice of actors and actions, i.e., subjects and verbs.

Sentences 5 through 9 present ghosts; readers only wonder "*Who did that*?" Remember, when readers encounter an information deficit, they fill in their own information, even if subconsciously. That's when you hear the comment, "I thought this meant. . ." Writers must not leave room for creative reading!

This is a Simple sentence—one subject and two verbs. Note: try to *avoid* separating the helping and main verb; instead of *was later implemented*, for Reader Comfort say "*was implemented later.*"

This sentence is Compound -- two independent clauses joined with a semicolon.

This sentence is Simple—one set of subject and verb (and two prep phrases at the end of the sentence).

We can't ask for more than pink, green, and blue!

5. **The XYZ system was developed as a pilot system (in January) and was later implemented (in its first field office) (in May). (S)**

Who did that? Must be the ghosts, or the gremlins? A better presentation uses the prep phrases as transitions to provide parallel introductions for the main points.

(In January,) staff developed the pilot XYZ system; (in July,) the department implemented it (in the first field office).(Cd)

or

In January, staff developed the pilot XYZ system (for July implementation) (in the first field office). (S)

These edits explain *who did what* very clearly. In addition, the color scheme reflects the clarity.

6. A determination <u>interview</u> <u>may need</u> to be performed (for eligibility). (S)

By whom, for whom? This sentence offers no identified actors. It fails to reveal *who does what.*

The <u>applicant</u> <u>may need</u> to prove eligibility (through a determination interview). (S)

The edit explains who does what; "applicant" is a much better actor than "interview."

The original and the edit both use the same weak verb construction, but it is the most appropriate; "may need" suggests the conditional aspect of the situation.

7. **These notices are sent (to the claimant and the employer). (S)**

Who does that? Who sends the notices? Recall that when the writer chooses a weak actor, one incapable of action, the verb is also weak. Unless you are not at liberty to reveal the actor, increase the readers' comfort by providing all the appropriate information:

Our staff sends these notices (to the claimant and the employer). (S)

Now the verb changes from orange to green; a strong actor performs a strong action!

If you choose to spotlight the claimant and the employer, the recipients, edit the sentence as follows:

The claimant and the employer receive these notices (from our staff). (S)

As the writer, you have total control of your actors and their actions. You choose who goes in the spotlight. What empowerment! Sadly, many business writers fail to take full advantage of this power.

Frequently we notice that yellow and orange have a natural affinity for each other.

Prep Phrases

pop up everywhere! In this sentence, prep phrases contain 70% of the word count. We must edit the yellow, the prep phrases that interrupt the S/V: *all...have been delivered*.

Maintain the opening prep phrase as a transition; it tells time. From the last prep phrase, draft *claims department* to actor/subject position; this invites a strong verb. Now the reader understands *who did what. Claims department* is a much stronger actor than *all*.

Reader Comfort increases tremendously, thereby increasing reader retention.

8. **(As of June 2), all (of the reports) [that are necessary (for recovery) (of the duplicate payments)] have been delivered (to the claims department). (Cx)**

Again, we have no idea who delivered *all*; moreover, *all* is such a weak actor that the writer needed three prep phrases and one dependent clause to define the subject word—certainly not a good sign!

At first glance you might think this sentence presents a formidable editing task; don't despair. Ask *who did what?* and aim to eliminate all the yellow–the prep phrases that interrupt everything. Note the clarity achieved with a few edits:

As of June 2, the claims department received all reports necessary to recover duplicate payments. (S)

We see no yellow now! This edit removes all the prep phrases and delivers the information in a more direct, more powerful presentation. Note that sentence construction changed from Cx to S, from two sets of S/V to one. Furthermore, word count decreases from 21 to 14, a 33% reduction.

9. **They were notified** and the correct **version was moved** (into production) (on July 15).   **(Cd)**

Even if we do not know *who* notified them, we *must* know who moved the correct version into production, unless that information is top secret. This sentence becomes more communicative if we change the opening, non-informative subject-verb to a prep phrase, move the last prep phrase to the front to establish time, and then insert a real actor capable of action; "version" is a weak actor that invites a weak verb.

(Upon notification) (on July 15,) Joe moved the correct version into production. (S)

Much better, don't you think?

Sentences 10-17 illustrate confusing subject-verb splits caused by prep phrases. Unnecessarily, the sentences reflect too much yellow (too many prep phrases); the writer failed to monitor Reader Comfort, and forgot that every sentence must tell *who did what*. The good news? These sentences edit easily if you adhere to The VanWrite Method. Watch this:

Sounds like a lot of work, but it goes quickly once you see the pattern, once you embrace the VanWrite Method for clarity. Perhaps the best aspect of this method is its consistency.

The two short opening prep phrases function as transitions; they set the stage and show the relationship between notification and the resulting action. In a Simple sentence now we enjoy the colors of clarity (and boys, girls, & money).

The ugly yellow and orange color scheme indicates big problems.

Concrete noun:

something you can see, touch, hold, or read, in this case *Attachment I*, as opposed to an abstract noun like "justice" or "honor."

Adjective:

describes nouns; what kind of results does *Attachment I* provide? *Analysis* results.

10. **The summary <u>results</u> (of this analysis) <u>are enclosed</u> (as Attachment I). (S)** ✓

Who does what? In this case, *results* perform no action, but *Attachment I* seems like a good candidate. Note the fantastic change in colors when we draft *Attachment I* as the actor:

Attachment I provides the summary analysis results. (S)

This edit makes the concrete noun, *Attachment I*, the actor; furthermore, this edit employs a strong verb that tells what *Attachment I* does, and it reduces the prep phrase to an adjective.

The opening dependent clause
works as a transition, and juxtaposes a strong subject with a
strong verb.

Maintain the opening dependent clause as a transition.

Remember—be lean and direct
and you'll communicate
directly to the reader's intellect.

Those amazing colors say it all!

11. [As the program evolves], continued discussions and research (by the parties) [who are involved] provide the means to. . . (Cx)

In the main/independent clause, the subject and verb suffer a long split because of the prep phrase and second dependent clause. Furthermore, the writer hid the breathing parties in the prep phrase. The reader feels uncomfortable and needs to read up the page to confirm *who does what.* Note how the edit makes the breathing parties the actor/subject; in addition, the edit eliminates the second dependent clause and other deadwood:

[As the program evolves,] the involved parties continue discussions and research to. . . (Cx)

Notice that we changed the second dependent clause to a one-word adjective! The wordy expression *provide the means to* adds no more than a plain *to.* These deletions cut length from 18 words to 12, a 33% reduction. As usual, fewer words make a stronger impression.

Is *responsibilities* a good actor? Why don't we use *Tom* as actor, you wonder? Good question! If I use *Tom* as actor, no doubt the verb will be very static--and the *responsibilities* will read like a prep phrase: *Under this program, Tom is responsible for. . .* Avoid telling your reader the obvious. We know Tom is responsible; otherwise he would not have this job.

12. Tom's <u>responsibilities</u> (under this program) include. . .

The fastest edit here suggests that we move the prep phrase to the beginning of the sentence; this allows us to juxtapose the subject and verb, yielding pink and green. Furthermore, the prep phrase itself goes from a yellow interrupter to a blue transition. Clearly, this edit strengthens the sentence:

(Under this program), Tom's <u>responsibilities</u> include. . .

Always try this approach
when you find a prep phrase
between S/V. You'll see that
many prep phrases reduce to
adjectives.

13. Implementation (of this program) provides. . .

To eliminate the prep phrase between the subject and verb, reduce the prep phrase to a one-word adjective and move it to the left of the subject:

Program implementation provides. . .

This edit provides the reader with a stronger hook to grab. As we discussed earlier, when you find yellow between S/V, be suspicious of the word in subject position; frequently that word is a lousy subject, evidenced by the need to support it with a prep phrase.

14. Our <u>approach</u> (to project management) <u>emphasizes</u>. . .

A few editing options exist here. If you choose to maintain *approach* in subject/actor position, then drop the preposition *to* and use *project management* as adjectives to the left of *approach*:

Our project management <u>approach</u> <u>emphasizes</u>. .

Some might question the value of *approach to,* wondering how those words contribute to understanding and Reader Comfort. Furthermore, *approach* isn't the strongest actor; it requires introduction or definition. With this in mind, try:

Our <u>project management emphasizes</u>. . .

This edit employs a stronger actor, one that distinguishes the topic more directly. Readers find it easier to identify *project management* than *approach.*

When you evaluate a sentence according to the VanWrite Method, you determine its strengths and weaknesses quickly.

15. While further <u>development</u> (of the program) continues. . .

For maximum clarity, reduce the prep phrase to a single-word adjective and move it to the left of the subject:

While further program <u>development</u> continues. . .

This edit changes the (obnoxious) yellow to (beautiful) pink.

The opening prep phrases function as transitions/stage-setters.

After the prep phrases in the original, the reader experiences difficulty determining the main focus because the writer included so many clauses, each with its own subject/topic.

Yellow Alert:

This S/V agreement error goes out of every office every day in the USA. When a prep phrase separates the S/V, the writer is fatally tempted to make the verb agree with the noun in the prep phrase instead of the noun in subject position.

16. **(Due to the magnitude) (of this systems project,) one (of our concerns) include ensuring [that proper channels are established] [through which information is received and reported.] (Cx)**

What a read-it-again struggle this presents! Note that the sentence contains only one very brief independent clause—*one include ensuring*; this independent clause follows two opening prep phrases, contains one prep phrase itself, and precedes two consecutive dependent clauses.

Note also the grave grammatical error within that short independent clause; the subject of the independent clause is weak, requiring a prep phrase to qualify or define it. However, that defining prep phrase caused a grammatical error; the writer made the verb *include* agree with the noun *concerns* rather than with the subject *one*. Bad news. The S/V should read *one includes* to be grammatically correct.

What can we do to reduce this 26-word sentence so it provides more Reader Comfort? In the clauses, the various grammatical subjects include *one*, *channel*s, and *information*; in other words, we have no humans in action here! *Who does what?* We do not know! Revision needs to include strong actors, and fewer

This juxtaposes the S/V, but
the verb is orange; however,
this auxiliary construction is
the one we use when we
express conditional situations.

We cannot overstate the danger
of separating subject and verb
with a prep phrase. Writers
have a strong tendency to
make the verb agree with the
prep phrase rather than with
the subject of the sentence.
This common error stems from
our poor choice of words in
subject position. Writers must
choose strong subjects that
require no interrupting definitions; those interrupters invite
grammatical errors.

Observation:

Subconsciously, writers want
to juxtapose subject and verb.
The evidence for this? The fre-
quency of S/V agreement
errors involving prep phrases.

dependent clauses. Study the following edit that col-
lapses the last two dependent clauses to infinitives:

> **(Due to the magnitude) (of this systems
> project,) we must establish proper channels
> to receive and to report information. (S)**

The revision lowers word count to 19, a 27% reduction. In a Simple sentence the reader focuses on only
one set of S/V. '

If you fret because the above edit does not include
the concept of *ensure*, try the following; note that the
message itself then goes into a dependent clause:

> **(Due to the magnitude) (of this systems
> project,) we must ensure [that we establish
> proper channels to receive and report infor-
> mation]. (Cx)**

Assume your boss insists that you use no orange—no auxiliary or helping (weak) verbs; in such a case, the edit reads:

(Due to the magnitude) (of this systems project,) our concerns include establishing proper channels to receive and to report information. (S)

This edit sacrifices the strong human actor, but it abolishes the orange.

This is your call to determine which edit speaks most clearly. Each suggestion improves the original tremendously!

Recall that yellow is **not** a pretty color in this arena.

This edit reduced word count 21%, from 19 to 15 words. The remaining prep phrase functions as a transition, changing the color scheme from lots of yellow to blue, pink, and green. There you go—rock 'n' roll! The VanWrite Method works every time!

17. **Involvement** (**of our staff**) (**through all the phases**) (**of development**) guarantees [**that your technical support team will be informed**]. (Cx)

Again, because *Involvement* is a vague subject, the writer used three prep phrases to qualify involvement; the verb follows nine words behind the subject! Moreover, the sentence does not tell *who does what* until the reader reorganizes the information mentally. Note the brevity achieved when we eliminate two prep phrases by reducing them to adjectives, and draft *staff* to actor/subject position:

(**Through all development phases,**) our **staff** guarantees [**that your technical support team will be informed**]. (Cx)

Isn't color an amazing addition to your editing? Never again will you see a sentence as only black and white! Instead, you will determine its quality according to the VanWrite colors of clarity and target editing.

Target Editing

Chapter **6**

Notes:

Use this area to make notes to yourself about these unclear sentences/passages.

Edit For Clarity
Poise Your Pens for Colorful Practice

Enjoy this opportunity to use your new editing skills. Identify the weaknesses in each of these passages. To insure the objectivity and to reinforce the methods we employed throughout the book, underline <u>subject</u> once, and <u>verb</u> twice; put (parentheses) around prep phrases, and [brackets] around dependent clauses. Then, with your pens, highlight areas appropriately. Finally, suggest edits for each passage to increase Reader Comfort. After you complete this practice, compare your findings to the suggested edits that follow this section. Have at it—and don't forget to ask *who did what!*

1. **The purpose of this memo is to provide each of you with both an explanation of the factors which caused and aggravated this problem, and to share with you our plans to provide some short-term relief.**

2. **There appears to be some confusion as to who can authorize spending.**

ARC = Appointment Review
Committee
PRE = Promotional Readiness
Evaluation

Whew! No Reader Comfort
exists here! The ghosts have
full control.

3.   Sacramento's abundance of parks provide a variety of recreational activities.

4.   It is impossible to put down all the possibilities of when one might grant vacation or when you should not grant it.

5.   Utilization of an ARC for classes below associate using the PRE report in a promotional examination is to be determined by Executive staff.

6.   The main objective of this project was to provide balances on critical projects in a timely manner ... Study after study done by our office, outside consulting firms, and auditors pointed to a need for an automated system to better control the billing function ... Susan is the person responsible in Administration for the billing of time charges and processing of expenses for our projects ... The billing system was shown to Susan and a balance report was produced ... The balances in the manual system Susan had maintained all these years and the balances of the data input into the automated system were compared.

7. A number of administrative functions are required in support of these activities.

8. We were able to determine that 18 of our original 24 recommendations which applied to Sacramento units have been satisfactorily met through the means of active compliance, change of circumstances, or lack of cost/benefit feasibility.

9. A state department which is interested in finding acceptable solutions to the operational problems of specific types of community self-help organizations recently sent two of its staff members to meet with one such organization.

10. The future well-being of our society, values, and ability to compete in the international marketplace are all largely dependent upon the development, welfare, and education of our children.

11. Although other parts of the state are experiencing nominal rates of growth and in some cases, declining rates of growth, Sacramento is

an area which is constantly luring major commercial business representation away from other parts of the state and other parts of the country as well.

12. There are also problems with the performance of the system and the reliability and timeliness of the information that is provided. The lack of confidence in the current system has led to a number of functions being performed manually and a higher degree of confidence in the manual system than in the automated system. . . . The new system will result in increased dependency on the automated system and less dependency on the manual system leading to increased productivity and lower costs.

Initially, your analysis should incorporate the demonstrated colors to reveal the weaknesses in each passage. Then, your edits for Reader Comfort should approximate the suggestions offered:

Isn't this a classic sample of bureaucratic rambling?

Unnecessary words and syllables always make a sentence babble; I liken it to noisy bubbles rising to the surface. or a mouth full of marbles.

Frequently, *-tion* nouns hide a good strong verb; how do you *provide an explanation*? Gift wrapped? Explain!

Notice that the edit reduces length from 37 to 14 words. a 62% decrease!

1. **The <u>purpose</u> of this memo <u>is</u> to provide each of you with both an explanation of the factors [which caused and aggravated this problem], and to share with you our plans to provide some short-term relief.**

Problems:

- Prepositional phrase between subject and verb
- Too many words/syllables
- Weak verb in independent clause
- Low Reader Comfort

Suggested edit:

This <u>memo explains</u> the problem's cause and our plans to provide short-term relief.

Rationale:

- Subject and topic become the same word.
- The verb presents the action accurately.
- The sentence tells *who did what* even though the *who* does not have a heartbeat.
- The *'s* lets me drop a prep phrase.

2. There <u>appears</u> to be some <u>confusion</u> as to [who can <u>authorize</u> spending.]

What does *appears to be* really mean? Does confusion exist, or not? Clue: *exists/exist* is a very handy synonym for *there is* or *there are* constructions.

Problems:

- Wordy and unclear
- Weak verb
- Low Reader Comfort

Suggested edit:

Confusion exists concerning spending authorization.

or

Confusion exists concerning [who may authorize spending].

Rationale:

- Drop *There* as a sentence opener because it begs for a weak verb and a wordy sentence.
- Second edit addresses permission issue with the use of *may*, while *can* referred to physical ability.
- Replaces the weak verb.

Sacramento's <u>abundance</u> of parks (provide) a variety of recreational activities.

Problems:

- Prep phrase between S/V invites the S/V agreement error; the verb should be *provides*.

- *abundance* is a weak actor that needs a prep phrase to qualify or define it; otherwise we ask, *abundance of what?*

Suggested edit:

Sacramento's many parks provide varied recreational activities.

Rationale:

- The edit identifies a concrete *who*, and juxtaposes S/V.

- The edit uses fewer words, and no prep phrases.

Note how we reduced *variety of* to *varied*, thereby eliminating the prep phrase. Recall our regular rule: reduce the prep phrase in whole or part to an adjective and move the adjective to the left of the noun/subject.

Again, this error occurs in every office every day; when writers separate subject and verb with a prep phrase, they provide fertile ground for a verb error. Writers have a subconscious desire to juxtapose S/V.

An alternative edit reads:

In Sacramento, many parks provide varied recreational activities. This edit uses the prep phrase *In Sacramento* as a transition (telling location).

It is provides the second most boring sentence opening, after *There is* or *There are*.

This sentence goes beyond revise; however, with target editing in mind, the writer rewrites with greater ease.!

In these suggested edits (rewrites!), even though the nouns in subject position lack heartbeats, they make much better actors than *It*. This comforts the reader, and thus increases comprehension.

4. **It is** impossible to put down all the possibilities of [when **one might grant** vacation] or [when **you should not grant** it.]

Problems:

- The weak, negative opening offers little Reader Comfort.
- The pronouns shift from third person (one) to second person (you).
- The dependent clauses present weak verbs.

Suggested edit:

Many considerations determine vacation scheduling.

or

Numerous reasons exist for granting or denying vacation.

Rationale:

- S/V relate to topic more specifically.
- Sentence becomes Simple rather than Complex with two dependent clauses.

5. **Utilization (of an ARC) (for classes) (below asso-ciate) using the PRE report (in a promotional examination) is to be determined (by Executive staff).**

Problems:

- Four prep phrases separate the subject and (weak) verb.

- Subject is a dead actor that requires a great deal of explanation, four prep phrases worth; the heartbeat appears in the last prep phrase.

Suggested edit:

Executive staff determines the use of an ARC with a PRE report in a promotional examina-tion.

or

In a promotional examination, Executive staff determines ARC utilization with a PRE report.

Rationale:

- Drafts the strong actor and a stronger form of an existing verb to S/V position; this answers *who does what.*

- Reduces prep phrases by at least 40%.

When they appear *after* the subject and verb, prep phrases pose less threat to Reader Comfort if you limit the number to three or fewer. Even so, seize every opportu-nity to collapse prep phrases to adjectives.

To break up the string of prep phrases, move one phrase to the front of the sentence to function as a transition.

Due to the length of this passage and the very weak color scheme, I model the revision process on the next page. I show you how to cross out deadwood and make targeted revisions. These revisions follow the VanWrite Method to increase clarity at the same time that you decrease word count.

6. The main objective of this project was to provide balances on critical projects in a timely manner. ... Study (after study) [done] by our office, outside consulting firms, and auditors pointed to a need (for an automated system) to better control the billing function. ... Susan is the person responsible (in Administration) (for the billing) (of time charges) and (processing of expenses) (for our projects). ... The billing system was shown to Susan and a balance report was produced. The balances in the manual system [Susan had maintained all these years] and the balances of the data [input into the automated system] were compared.

Problems:

- Ghosts dominate!
- Four times, prep phrases separate S/V.
- The passage contains seven additional prep phrases.
- We find only one strong verb.
- In the first sentence, the subject and topic clash.

In Administration puts the prep phrase first to establish location. If Susan were the office robot we would identify her as such; since she is a person, skip the announcement! Don't tell us she is responsible; show us what she does.

The vendor gives us a strong actor.

In the last very lengthy sentence in the original, the subjects are balances and balances, and the verb is were compared. The edit reveals who did what.

Suggested edit: (work in progress)

~~The main objective of~~ This project ~~was to~~ ✓ provided *timely* balances on critical projects ~~in a timely manner.~~ ... *Several* Stud~~y~~ies ~~after study~~ (indicated) a need for an automated *billing* system. ~~to better control the billing function.~~ ... In Administration, Susan ~~is the person responsible in Administration for the~~ (billings) ~~of~~ time charges and (processinges) ~~of~~ expenses for our projects. ... *The* vendor showed The billing system ~~was shown~~ to Susan and (produced) a balance report ~~was produced~~. ✓ Then Susan (compared) the *manual* balances ~~in the manual system Susan had maintained all these years and~~ with the *automated* balances. ~~of the data input into the automated system were compared~~

Whack and Slash—

Note the increased Reader Comfort provided by this whack-and-slash edit. Now the reader easily follows the logic and the sequence of events.

Suggested edit: (final product)

This **project** ***provided*** timely balances on critical projects. ... Several **studies** ***indicated*** a need for an automated billing system. **In Administration**, **Susan** (**bills**) time charges and processes expenses for our projects. ... The **vendor** ***showed*** the billing system to Susan and ***produced*** a balance report. **Then Susan** ***compared*** the manual balances with the automated balances.

Rationale

- Every sentence tells *who did what.*
- The revision deletes fifty-four words, a 53% reduction in text.
- The colors improve dramatically!

7. A **number** (of administrative functions) **are required** (in support) (of these activities). ✓

Problems:

- A prep phrase separates subject and verb.
- The word in subject position is weak/too vague; it requires a prep phrase of explanation.
- The topic—*these activities*—appears in the last prep phrase.

Suggested edit:

These **activities require** administrative support.

Rationale:

- The topic becomes the grammatical subject.
- The revision uses a strong present-tense verb.
- The revision eliminates all three prep phrases.
- The revision reduces word count by 59%, from twelve words to five.

Remember, in these leaner years, less is more; your writing commands more attention and respect if you use fewer words.

Talk about a lack of Reader Comfort. This passage requires several re-readings— ban the yellow!

In this complicated Complex sentence, the independent clause contains no real information; all the news hides in the lengthy dependent clause.

8. ✓
    We were able to determine [that **18** (of our original 24 recommendations) [which applied (to Sacramento units)] **have been** satisfactorily **met** (through the means) (of active compliance, (change of circumstances), or (lack of cost/benefit feasibility.)]

Problems:

- The independent clause provides no information, and includes a weak verb structure.

- Sentence length exceeds 28 words; Reader Comfort recommends 18-22 words.

- In the dependent clause, the subject (*18*) and verb (*have been satisfactorily met*) are separated by a prep phrase *and another* dependent clause containing *another* prep phrase!

- A ghost dominates the dependent clause—who performed these actions?

Suggested edit:

Of our original 24 recommendations regarding Sacramento units, Department X met 18 satisfactorily through active compliance, change of circumstances, or lack of cost/benefit feasibility.

Rationale:

- Eliminates the opening independent clause as it says nothing.

- Begins the sentence with the first prep phrase to set the scene or establish the situation.

- Identifies an actor—explains *who did what.*

Come again? What is the point here? The reader has to underline and paint just to get a clue! Ahhh ... aren't these colors bright? Unfortunately, bright is not right.

The revised color scheme reflects a vast increase in Reader Comfort.

9. A **company** [which is interested (in finding acceptable solutions) (to the operational problems) (of specific types) (of community self-help organizations)] recently (sent) two (of its staff members) to meet (with one such organization.)

Problems:

- A 19-word dependent clause separates subject and verb; the dependent clause contains four lengthy prep phrases.

- The reader does not know if the *company* went to seek answers, or to provide solutions. The ambiguity frustrates the reader.

Suggested edit:

A **company** (sent) two staff members to meet with a community self-help organization to find solutions to the organization's operational problems.

Rationale:

- The revision juxtaposes subject and verb to explain *who did what*.

- The total prep phrase count drops from six to two.

10. The future <u>well-being</u> (of our society, values, and ability to compete) (in the international marketplace) <u>are</u> all largely dependent (upon the development, welfare and education) (of our children).

Problems:

- The subject/verb agreement error results from the two prep phrases between the subject and the weak verb; *well-being* is a singular concept.

- The sentence contains too many ideas, and most of the ideas hide in prep phrases.

Reader Comfort plummets as the reader juggles all the abstract terms.

Suggested edit:

Our children's <u>welfare and education determine</u> our society's values and ability to compete internationally.

Rationale:

- The subjects and the verb become juxtaposed. *Welfare* and *education* define *well-being* more specifically.

- A stronger verb replaces the boring *are*.

11. [Although other <u>parts</u> (of the state) <u>are experiencing</u> nominal rates (of growth) and (in some cases), declining rates (of growth)], **Sacramento is** an area [which <u>is</u> constantly <u>luring</u> major commercial business representation away (from other parts) (of the state) and other parts (of the country) as well.]

Problems:

- The sentence contains 46 words! The reader feels quite confused at the end.

- The independent clause reads *Sacramento is an area*; no kidding! Give the reader some real news.

- The seven prep phrases become very monotonous and confusing.

Suggested edit:

[Although some **California areas experience** nominal or declining growth rates,] **Sacramento continues** to lure major state and national commercial businesses.

And on and on and on—enough! Ugly color scheme, of course. . .

Rationale:

- The edit yields a 19-word sentence.

- Several prep phrases reduce to single-word adjectives.

- The opening dependent clause presents the negative news, but the independent clause counters the bad news and promotes the topic, *Sacramento*, which also serves as the grammatical subject.

- Word count decreases 59% and the repetition disappears.

Here's that boring sentence opening again.

In this passage the color scheme says it all.

12. **There are also problems (with the perfor-mance) (of the system) and the reliability and timeliness (of the information) [that is pro-vided]. The lack (of confidence) (in the current system) has led (to a number) (of functions) being performed manually and a higher degree (of confidence) (in the manual system) than (in the automated system)... The new system will result (in increased dependency) (on the auto-mated system) and less dependency (on the manual system) (leading to increased produc-tivity and lower costs).**

Problems:

- This passage contains far too many weak verbs and prep phrases.

- The passage includes NO human actors!

- In the second sentence the grammatical subject is weak, evidenced by the two prep phrases that follow to explain *lack*.

- The last sentence reflects poor word choice; in our culture, we strive to increase *confidence*, not *dependency*. Furthermore, the last line ignores the importance of parallel construction and natural pairs; when you *increase* produc-tivity, you *decrease* costs. Alternately, you *raise* productivity and *lower* costs. Reader Comfort demands attention to such details.

These colors please both the eye and the intellect.

Suggested edit:

Problems exist with the performance, reliability, and timeliness of the current system. Lacking confidence in the automated system, staff performs many functions manually. The new system will generate confidence in automation; in turn, this confidence will increase productivity and decrease costs.

Rationale:

- The edit sharply reduces the number of prep phrases.
- The edit juxtaposes subject and verb in every sentence.
- The edit includes future tense verbs, but this is a proposal for future action.

Bravo! You just completed this editing practice. Review these edits frequently until you feel comfortable with the VanWrite Method. Once you find your balance with the concepts, they become as automatic as riding a bike, and you will target edit with greater ease, confidence, and clarity.

Target Editing

Chapter 7

Eclectic:
the best from diverse sources.

Why worry
so much about Reader Comfort? A comfortable reader tends to offer much less resistance to your message. A comfortable reader agrees with the writer. A comfortable reader focuses on your message instead of becoming distracted by poor writing that fails to communicate. Reader Comfort increases comprehension, a goal of all good business writers.

VanWrite Revisions at Work
A Review of How-to

As promised in Chapter 1, the last three chapters present no new information. In this final chapter we look at an eclectic collection of original, quite wordy business sentences. Then we revise using the VanWrite Method to exhibit new strengths. Before we begin, study the following summary of our major goals that insure clarity in written expression.

VanWrite Editing Goals:

- Always think about **Reader Comfort!**

- Make sure every sentence answers *who did what.*

- Put a strong actor in subject position whenever possible. Look for potential actors hidden in the prep phrase:

     ✓
This **memo** **should be read** (by all staff members.)

becomes
     ✓
All **staff members** **should read** this memo.

- Juxtapose subject and verb; avoid prep phrases or other interference between subject and verb (S/V).

- If you find a prep phrase between subject and verb, collapse the phrase to an adjective and/or move the phrase to the left of the subject.

Members (of the Board) spoke last night.

becomes

Board members spoke last night.

- Use strong verbs to energize your writing and hold the readers' interest.

- Keep sentences under 22 words.

- Use transitions within and between paragraphs.

- Never begin a sentence with *It* or *There*—these words beg for boring verbs.

When a passage or document seems difficult to understand, first underline every subject and verb in pen or pencil. Then get your colors out and start painting until you discover the problem—weak verbs, S/V splits, no transitions, repetitious sentence style, lengthy sentences, poor unity ... After you identify the problem(s), prioritize your editing according to **Reader Comfort**.

Members is vague—members of what? *Board members* allows no confusion.

Priority editing—

Prioritize your editing according to Reader Comfort; first, address those passages that most confuse the reader. Always strive to eliminate all yellow since yellow distracts the reader. You want to replace yellow with pink to reflect juxtapositioning of S/V. Aim to replace 60-70% of your orange checks with green circles. Finally, make sure you have a comfortable amount of blue to transition the reader through your thoughts.

Questionable Subject Word:

When you find several words between S/V, the subject word is probably weak or vague: the S needs to be defined, qualified or limited before the writer continues.

Unfortunately, we read, and unwittingly write, this kind of stuff daily. Perhaps imprecise wordy writing results from wordy speech patterns.

Remember, the VanWrite Method follows regular, predictable, objective guidelines. Once you internalize the concepts of strong grammatical subjects, subject-verb juxtapositioning, prep phrase editing/reduction, strong verbs, and transitions, you handle each editing task with ease and grace. If you find lots of verbiage (i.e., garbage) between subject and verb, always question the word in subject position. Then look at the verb. Finally, ask *who does what?*

Realize that all of the following examples are authentic sentences that participants brought to our seminars. Note the contrast between the original wordy, lazy presentation and the shorter, stronger, VanWrite edit that increases clarity.

- **The __office__ [where he works] __is__ miles (from his house). (Cx)**

This sentence is unnecessarily Cx; note, too, that the dependent clause separates the S/V of the main/independent clause. *Who does what?*

He works miles (from home). (S)

or

He works (in an office) miles (from home).

Both revisions yield Simple, shorter sentences.

- **AIDS is** a disease [that kills]. (Cx)

Now that's a flash! Tell it like it is.

AIDS kills. (S)

If the audience doesn't know that AIDS is a disease, you probably have very little reason to communicate anyway.

- **Sue is** the woman [who answers customer complaints]. (Cx)

If this person's gender is a major issue, then discuss it in the independent clause; if, however, that is not a concern, skip ahead to *who does what*, and eliminate the dependent clause.

Sue answers customer complaints. (S)

Same song, different verse:

- **John is** the person [who trains new employees]. (Cx)

If John were the company robot, we would need to be told about the robotic approach to training. Since

The edit from Cx to S decreases word count by 50%, and increases Reader Comfort 100%!

Ditto word count decrease!
So sweet in this hectic work
world.

Remember, *-ing* words are not
verbs unless they are preceded
by a form of *To Be* as in *are
walking, was running, is thinking.* Furthermore, *-ing* words
are bor-ing!

Occasionally, debate occurs
over expressions like *My staff.*
Instead, some managers prefer
a less authoritarian reference,
such as *Our team. Our staff,*
or *We.*

Good colors—three green
verbs!

The first two sentences work
well in a paragraph on *dimensions.* In a paragraph on the
office, the third sentence

John is just an ordinary person, skip any announce-ment of the obvious. Simply put:

John trains new employees. (S)

- **My staff is responsible (for writing, editing, and distributing the quarterly report). (S)**

Why is it necessary to mention the concept of *responsibility?* Isn't that a given when people work—that they bear responsibility? All the real information hides in a prep phrase with boring *-ing* non-verbs. Note the clarity when we ask *who does what?*

My staff writes, edits, and distributes the quarterly report. (S)

The edit makes the staff sound pro-active and capable; the reader forms mental images of this group in action. Furthermore, the edit reduced word count by 25%, from 12 to 9 words.

- **The dimensions (of the office) are 8' x 9'. (S)**

Recall the question you ask yourself when a prep phrase separates subject and verb; what is the weak-ness in the subject that requires a prep phrase of

reflects clarity. Recall that the word in subject position should reflect the topic of that sentence in particular, as well as the topic of the paragraph in general.

definition? *Dimensions* needs to be pinpointed or located. In this sentence we have two editing alternatives. One approach suggests that we reduce the prep phrase to an adjective and move it to the left of the subject word:

The office dimensions are 8' x 9'. (S)

This eliminates the prep phrase, the yellow, so that the subject and verb are now juxtaposed, pink. However, the verb remains weak, orange. Even if the *who* does not have a heartbeat, the sentence is stronger if the subject is concrete and the verb is active. What do dimensions *do?* They measure!

The office measures 8' x 9'. (S)

- **A fire was discovered [while I was walking (down the road)]. (Cx)**

Who discovered the fire? The reader might supply the wrong actor. How's this for wordy, passive, noncommittal? *Fire* does not do anything other than burn, so the verb has to be passive.

[While I walked (down the road)], I discovered a fire. (Cx)

As in most Cx sentences, the clauses may be reversed to maximize Reader Comfort. You determine what you need based on the style of other sentences in the paragraph. You want to avoid lulling the reader with any single sentence style.

In these two sentences, the grammatical subject is *you*, the only implied grammatical subject we have in English. If I say, *Answer the phone!*, the subject is *you* and the verb is *answer*.

Although this sentence offers pink and green in the dependent clause, the reader experiences a glitch due to the S/V split within the independent clause.

Now the dependent clause functions as a transition, and the independent clause tells *who did what.*

- **Enclosed please (find) the actuarial chart. (S)**

Sure... no problem! Now what? This sentence fails to direct or instruct the reader; the reader must act as a mind reader to determine what the writer wants. Anytime the writer leaves room for interpretation, the writer must expect that the reader could arrive at an incorrect response. A better sentence creates a mindset and tells the reader what to do:

Please (study) the enclosed actuarial chart to understand our rates. (S)

Now the reader brings expectations to the chart and can self-educate. The sentence is much more communicative.

- **The flowers [that grow here] were planted (by my manager). (Cx)**

This Cx sentence features an embedded dependent clause that separates the subject and passive verb in the independent clause; since flowers do not do anything, they require a passive verb. Also, the breathing actor hides in a prep phrase at the end of the sentence. Revised, *who did what* yields:

My manager planted these flowers. (S)

The 10-word Cx sentence reduces 50% to a five-word Simple sentence, and displays the colors of clarity.

- **The following is a list (of projects) [that our staff completed last quarter]. (Cx)**

No doubt the reader sees the list, so why announce its presence? Furthermore, the presence of the list is not the major issue here; staff accomplishments is the point, yet that concept hides in the dependent clause. To highlight the staff, write a Simple sentence that tells *who did what:*

Our staff completed the following projects last quarter. (S)

This edit shrinks the sentence 39%, from 13 words to eight. With only one set of subject and verb, the reader maintains focus easily. To show chronology in an annual report, the writer might choose to use *last quarter* as a transition:

Optional edit:
My manager planted the flowers that grow here. (Cx)
However, why be unnecessarily complex?

Last quarter, our staff completed the following projects.

This edit simply repositions the time reference, and it provides a structure for presenting the other quarters.

- **There are no off-the-shelf materials available for this training. (S)**

Recall that the best synonym for *There are* is *exist*.

Remember, weak writers use a lot of words to support weak verbs. Note the subject/verb split caused by this awkward, but common, construction. *There* demands explanation since it is such a boring presentation. Cut to the chase!

No off-the-shelf materials exist for this training. (S)

This edit compresses the sentence and juxtaposes the subject and verb.

- **It is estimated [that about forty workdays of development time will be required to develop and refine this project]. (Cx)**

Who did/said that? The ghosts, no doubt! The independent clause tells us nothing; the news appears

Less is best!

This edit provides a sterling example of whack-whack-whack editing.

How sweet it is—

in wonderful colors, easy revisions increase clarity in your writing and success in your business transactions. Remember, boys, girls, and money. . .

in the wordy, clumsy, redundant dependent clause. This sentence presents too much orange and yellow to allow Reader Comfort. A couple of options exist to minimize the word count in this sentence:

We estimate about forty workdays to develop and refine this project. (S)

To achieve this brevity, we simply inserted a strong actor *We*, changed the form of the existing verb *estimated* to *estimate*, dropped the subordinating conjunction *that*, and eliminated the prep phrase *of development time* because the infinitive *to develop* expresses that thought.

If you think you need to address the *will be required* issue more directly, insert *needing* between *estimate* and *about*:

We estimate needing about forty workdays to develop and refine this project. (S)

By now you should feel comfortable with the predictable objectivity of the VanWrite Method. You begin to look at any sentence and visualize its components in vivid colors, either for the good or the weak. If you picture the weak colors, ask *who did what* to convert the orange and yellow to blue, pink and green. VanWrite revisions work well at work.

Afterword

Now that you have added six colorful pens to your writing toolkit, no sentence escapes your comprehension or scrutiny. As you strive for Reader Comfort, the VanWrite Method works for you when you plan what you want to write, as you proofread your own writing, and as you edit staff writing. You visualize the colors as you read and write in black and white. When you edit others' writing, no longer do you stammer when someone asks you why you made a particular edit.

Writers rarely intend to write a sentence that fails to communicate; however, if writers do not bring objective, measurable standards to their sentences, they face pot luck regarding the outcome. The VanWrite Method eliminates the pot luck. All writers are capable of clear expression if they make sure every sentence tells *who did what*, and they juxtapose a strong actor with a strong verb.

Furthermore, the VanWrite Method enables you to ask targeted questions about the writing that comes into your office as you try to ascertain the writer's message.

Quickly you determine if the writer gave you the right information for you to act or make a decision. Remember, weak writing reflects weak thinking; if you cannot determine the **who**, the **did**, and the **what** in a document, the writer failed to communicate. Your Reader Comfort is low.

Writers ask me frequently if they should write the way they talk. I tell them to talk to me for several minutes and I'll let them know! Seriously, the idea that we should write the way we talk gained popularity several years ago. Unfortunately, many people embraced the idea enthusiastically without giving thought to the way they talk. Hence, we see written sentences in excess of 40 words with the subject and verb separated by 12 words and three prep phrases. These constructions might communicate in spoken language because we have the benefits of voice inflection, body language, timing, and eye contact. However, they make for a rough ride in written communication; these are the sentences that cause the reader to put a finger on the period and go searching for the capital letter to reread.

Everybody moves at a fast pace these days, and we are all very busy. As a business writer, you have only a limited amount of time to complete each writing task and to make sure your sentences communicate easily. If you follow the VanWrite Method, you edit with clear targets to energize your business writing.

Target Editing

Appendix A

Subject and Object Pronouns

Many speakers and writers confuse pronouns in their communications. Successful business writers need full control over pronouns. A few very regular rules apply to correct pronoun use. Study these charts and the following examples to demystify pronouns forever.

Subject pronouns perform the action.

Subject pronouns follow any form of the verb *Be*.

Subject Pronouns		
Person	**Singular**	**Plural**
1st	I	we
2nd	you	you
3rd	he, she, it who	they who

Object Pronouns		
Person	**Singular**	**Plural**
1st	me	us
2nd	you	you
3rd	him, her, it whom	them whom

Object pronouns receive the action.

Object pronouns follow prepositions.

Subject Pronouns

Person	Singular	Plural
1st	I	we
2nd	you	you
3rd	he, she, it	they
	who	who

Subject pronouns perform the action.

Subject pronouns follow any form of the verb *Be*.

Object Pronouns

Person	Singular	Plural
1st	me	us
2nd	you	you
3rd	him, her, it	them
	whom	whom

Object pronouns receive the action.

Object pronouns follow prepositions.

Study the following sentences to understand the correct pronoun selection; the correct pronoun appears in italics.

1. **Bob gave his stamp collection to Rick and I/*me*.**

In Rick's absence, you would say, *Bob gave his stamp collection to **me**.* The object pronoun is correct here because this sentence involves receiving something.

2. **Sherry would like someone to drive Jody and she/*her* home.**

Again, if Jody were not there, this sentence would pose no problems; the presence or absence of another person does not affect pronoun selection! Sherry receives a ride.

3. ***We*/Us musicians have sensitive ears.**

If you skip the qualifier *musicians*, the choice is obvious; furthermore, *We* is in subject/actor position.

Subject Pronouns

Person	Singular	Plural
1st	I	we
2nd	you	you
3rd	he, she, it	they
	who	who

Subject pronouns perform the action.

Subject pronouns follow any form of the verb *Be*.

Object Pronouns

Person	Singular	Plural
1st	me	us
2nd	you	you
3rd	him, her, it	them
	whom	whom

Object pronouns receive the action.

Object pronouns follow prepositions.

4. The winner is *he*/him.

We always use subject pronouns after any form of the verb *Be*. Another reliable test suggests that you turn the statement around: *He* is the winner.

5. Nobody works harder than *they*/them.

Who works hard? *They* work hard. Another test is to finish the pronoun with a verb: Nobody works harder than *they* do.

6. Who/*Whom* did the club elect as treasurer?

Turn this question into a statement: The club elected *him* (or *her*). This test determines that you need an object pronoun.

7. Those are the people to *whom*/who Mrs. Green sold her car.

The *people* received Mrs. Green's car, so the pronoun needs to be objective. Put another way, Mrs. Green sold her car to *them*; since *them* is an object pronoun we use the equivalent *whom*. Also, we always use object pronouns after prepositions.

Subject Pronouns

Person	Singular	Plural
1st	I	we
2nd	you	you
3rd	he, she, it	they
	who	who

Subject pronouns perform the action.

Subject pronouns follow any form of the verb *Be*.

Object Pronouns

Person	Singular	Plural
1st	me	us
2nd	you	you
3rd	him, her, it	them
	whom	whom

Object pronouns receive the action.

Object pronouns follow prepositions.

8. Jennifer will play chess with whomever/*whoever* asks her.

In this sentence, the pronoun is in subject position in the dependent clause, so we need a subject pronoun, *whoever*. When the pronoun functions as a subject in the sentence, we must use a subject pronoun. Here, *with* is not a preposition; instead, it is functioning as a subordinating conjunction that signals a dependent clause.

9. *Who*/Whom did you say borrowed my meeting notes?

Answer the question! The pronoun is in subject position so we would say, *He* (or *she*) borrowed my notes. Another tactic—eliminate *did you say*; now the sentence reads, *Who* borrowed my meeting notes? *Who* is in subject position, so we need a subject pronoun.

10. Kevin will ask whoever/*whomever* he likes to the party.

Who will Kevin ask? Kevin will ask *them* (or *him* or *her*). These people will receive Kevin's invitation! Hence, we need an object pronoun.

Target Editing

Appendix **B**

As usual, use this area to make notes to yourself or to record questions.

VanWrite Color Code:

To review—
Pink   = S/V juxtaposed
Yellow = Prep phrase between S/V
Green = Strong verb
Orange= Weak verb
Blue   = Transitions

Sentence Classification Practice

This exercise provides additional practice with **S, Cd,** and **Cx** sentence classification. To restate a point from the end of Chapter 2, our study of sentence classification is quite cursory, by design. Academicians might consider our discussion too simplified; I call it simply relevant to the work setting.

Business writers have no survival need to study sentence construction as a grammarian would; however, business writers do need to understand clause, phrase, and sentence types well enough to make intelligent choices regarding actors/grammatical subjects. Business writers must be sensitive to the impact that subject selection has on Reader Comfort. Periodically review the discussion in Chapter 2 about the rationale for sentence construction variety.

Label each of the following sentences appropriately, using the editing indicators we have employed throughout our study: S̲, V̲, (prep phrase), [dependent clause], and the colors. Then study the suggested answers on the following pages.

This additional practice focuses on sentence classification. Do not worry about orange verbs or think you need to revise the verbs to green. Rather, identify the elements, and then study them to determine the sentence style.

Remember, if you find only one set of <u>subject</u> and <u>verb</u>, the sentence has to be Simple. If you find two sets of S/V, the sentence is either Compound or Complex, depending on the conjunction. If you have a coordinating conjunction (*and, but, or*) you have a Cd sentence. If you have a subordinating conjunction, you have a Cx sentence.

Recall that a phrase does NOT have both subject and verb; a clause has BOTH subject and verb. An independent clause stands alone; a dependent clause depends on an independent clause.

_____ 1. He spoke to us many times while he was in town.

_____ 2. We need to begin as soon as possible.

_____ 3. We will wait for your response before we choose a vendor.

_____ 4. Leaving Chicago, we enjoyed a majestic sunset.

_____ 5. As we left Chicago, we enjoyed a majestic sunset.

_____ 6. I will call you as soon as I return to the plant.

_____ 7. I expect to be promoted, but I am nervous about it.

_____ 8. This is an interesting article; it should be read by all staff members.

_____ 9. While we were in a meeting, one customer called to double his order.

_____ 10. I went to the office early and typed the report.

_____ 11. I went to the office early and I typed the report.

_____ 12. When I went to the office early, I typed the report.

_____ 13. Just as we sat down to dinner, we had a power failure.

_____ 14. We walked through the door, and the phone rang.

_____ 15. Some people like office jobs, but others prefer to work outdoors.

_____ 16. From the top of the building we enjoyed a great view of the parade.

_____ 17. We began our session when all the participants arrived.

_____ 18. The computers that sit here connect to the color printer.

_____ 19. The client who called after lunch was very upset.

_____ **20. At noon I turned off the computer, locked the doors, and left for a leisurely lunch.**

The following pages discuss each sentence and demonstrate the color scheme. If your answers differ significantly, please review the discussion of sentence construction in Chapter 2; when you have control of sentence style, you have control of your presentation in every sentence you write.

__Cx__ 1. He spoke (to us) many times [while he was (in town).]

__S__ 2. We need to begin (as soon as possible).

__Cx__ 3. We will wait (for your response) [before we choose a vendor.]

__S__ 4. Leaving Chicago, we enjoyed a majestic sunset.

__Cx__ 5. [As we left Chicago,] we enjoyed a majestic sunset.]

__Cx__ 6. I will call you [as soon as I return (to the plant).]

Re #1—independent clause first, then dependent; prep phrases do not interfere with S/V juxtapositioning.

Re #2—one independent clause, S/V juxtaposed , an infinitive, and a prep phrase telling when.

Re #3—much like #1; independent clause, dependent clause, prep phrase causes no grief.

Re #4—only one set of S/V means it's gotta be Simple!

Re #5—dependent clause first, separated from the independent by a comma.

Re #6—just like #1 with the prep phrase in the dependent clause. _as soon as_ becomes dependent conjunction due to presence of subject and verb, _I return._

Re #7—two complete sentences (independent clauses) joined by coordinating conjunction.

Re #8—two independent clauses joined by a semicolon.

Re #9—dependent clause with a prep phrase, independent clause. S/V juxtaposed in both.

Re #10—one subject and two verbs: has to be Simple with one subject.

Re #11—two independent clauses joined by a coordinating conjunction.

Re #12—dependent clause (S/V but not a complete thought) first, then independent clause.

Re #13—dependent clause, independent clause.

Re #14—two complete thoughts (independent clauses) joined by a coordinating conjunction.

Re #15—Again, two independent clauses joined by a coordinating conjunction.

Cd 7. I expect to be promoted, but I am nervous about it.

Cd 8. This is an interesting article; it should be read (by all staff members).

Cx 9. [While we were (in a meeting),] one customer called to double his order.

S 10. I went (to the office) early and typed the report.

Cd 11. I went (to the office) early, and I typed the report.

Cx 12. [When I went (to the office) early,] I typed the report.

Cx 13. [Just as we sat down to dinner,] we had a power failure.

Cd 14. We walked (through the door), and the phone rang.

Cd 15. Some people like office jobs, but others prefer to work outdoors.

Re #16—one set of S/V, three prep phrases; note how first two function as transitions.

Re #17—independent clause, dependent clause; no comma when independent is first.

Re #18—embedded/internal dependent clause; avoid this construction because it always separates S/V of main clause.

Re #19—another embedded dependent clause; note how it separates S/V of main clause, not a good idea in longer sentences because it reduces Reader Comfort.

Re #20—one actor/subject and three strong verbs. To be Compound we need a subject (actor) with each verb: *I locked, and I left* .

S 16. (From the top) (of the building) we enjoyed a great view (of the parade).

Cx 17. We began our session [when all the participants arrived.]

Cx 18. The computers [that sit here] connect (to the color printer).

Cx 19. The client [who called] (after lunch) was very upset.

S 20. (At noon) I turned off the computer, locked the doors, and left for a leisurely lunch.

Target Editing

Appendix **C**

Startled by the number of weak verbs they found in their business writing, two VanWrite students quickly compiled this list of strong verbs.   In their documents, they substituted one of these verbs for every boring verb they found.

Understand that this list is far from complete; rather, it serves to inspire you to reduce the orange and feature the green.

Strong Verbs for Business Writing

accept	define	force
address	denote	formulate
advise	derive	forward
affirm	describe	
agree	deserve	gain
analyze	design	garner
appreciate	designate	gauge
approach	determine	glean
appropriate	develop	govern
arrange	drive	gravitate
assist		grow
augment	educate	guide
authorize	emphasize	
	encourage	happen
capture	enhance	harness
collect	establish	highlight
communicate	evaluate	hinder
compile	examine	hold
compliment	exchange	
concur	expose	identify
conduct		implement
contrive	facilitate	improve
cooperate	factor	incorporate
coordinate	favor	initiate
cultivate	find	instigate
	focus	

institute   present   stress
interact   prevent   study
                   produce   submit
juggle   propose   summarize
justify   provide   support

launch   qualify   take
lead   quantify   terminate
leverage   query   track
liken   question   trust

manage   range   value
mediate   rank   verify
meet   recognize   veto
meter   recommend   voice
migrate   reiterate
muster   report   wield
                   require   work
obtain   resolve
offer   restate   yield
optimize   reveal
organize   revise

parcel   serve
participate   shape
perform   span
plan   sponsor
prepare   streamline

Suggested References

American Heritage Dictionary of the English Language. 3rd ed. Boston: Houghton Mifflin, 1992.

Merriam-Webster's Collegiate Dictionary. 10th ed. Springfield: Merriam-Webster, Inc., 1994.

The Merriam-Webster Concise Handbook for Writers. Springfield: Merriam-Webster Inc., 1991.

The Merrian-Webster Dictionary of English Usage. Springfield: Merrian-Webster Inc., 1989.

Roget's International Thesaurus. 5th ed. New York: HarperCollins, 1992.

Shartzer, Margaret. *The Elements of Grammar.* New York: Macmillan Publishing, 1986.

Strunk Jr., William and E. B. White. *The Elements of Style.* 3rd ed. New York: Macmillan Publishing, 1979.

Target Editing

Index **I**

Target Editing focuses on six easy principles that energize business writing. The book does not bog you down with academic discussions concerning minute grammar points. Instead, it arms you with powerful editing techniques that take the guesswork out of revising.

VanWrite Seminars

Linda Vanderwold, "Ms. VanWrite," delivers animated, informative, humorous seminars on business writing. If your company or organization would like to learn more about these seminars, contact VanWrite Writing Consultants at VanWrite@aol.com or write P.O. Box 4414, Davis, CA 95617-4414, or call (800) 800-0898. She presents seminars in various formats, based upon your organization's needs.

Note the comments of some former seminar participants:

"VanWrite seminars have value for any organization that places a premium on clear written expression. The VanWrite Method makes sense because it is so objective. Staff quickly learn how to make significant concrete edits that decrease writing time and increase their confidence in the final product."

Kevin Bacon
Principal, Price Waterhouse LLP

"Each year hundreds of VanWrite evaluations cross my desk because Linda is the most requested independent contractor for the State of California's State EDP Education Program (SEEP). Consistently Linda earns excellent reviews because professionals see immediate applicability and value in the writing method she presents in this book."

Karen Jackson
Manager, SEEP
State of California

"I give VanWrite seminars two thumbs up! The method is fun to learn and easy to remember. Linda's program provided a great boost for my staff. Even skeptics became champions of the VanWrite Method."

John Nitti
Western Area Director of Market Support
Software AG of North America, Inc.

"I have not seen, heard, or been with a better instructor."

John Zuniga, Jr.
Chief, Communications and Technical Support
California Environmental Protection Agency